Secrets to Affordable Antiques

How to Buy More for Less!

FRANK FARMER LOOMIS IV

©2004 Frank Farmer Loomis IV

Published by

Our toll-free number to place an order or obtain
a free catalog is (800) 258-0929.

krause publications

An imprint of F+W Publications, Inc.

700 East State Street • Iola, WI 54990-0001
715-445-2214 • 888-457-2873
www.krause.com

Library of Congress Catalog Number:

2004103294

ISBN:

0-87349-841-0

Designed by Sandy Kent

Edited by Dan Brownell

Printed in the United States of America

DEDICATION

To my mother, Jean Whitehouse Loomis,
who gave me her Grannie Taylor's Carnival
Glass, and whose love is ever in my heart.

Frank Farmer Loomis IV

TABLE *of* CONTENTS

FOREWORD

"In his comprehensive overview of the collecting and care of antiques, Frank Farmer Loomis IV presents an expansive and thoughtful insight of the American experience of collecting. Drawing on an impressive array of his own experiences, the author has written a concise, interesting, and important book, one that should interest a broad range of individuals."

Wendell Garrett
Senior Vice President, Sotheby's
Editor, *The Magazine Antiques*
Antiques Roadshow Appraiser

ACKNOWLEDGMENTS

These acknowledgments are my Dedication, Part Two, to these beloved people:

First, Ann Brandt and William Santen Sr., who both helped open a door of opportunity leading to this book. Thanks to my literary agent, Gail Newman, for her faith and work. Wonderful Karen Plunkett-Powell worked to the very end of her too short life editing this primer. How lucky I am to have my life enriched by Dianne Marcus, who aided me through the proposal and early drafts of this book and, of course, her husband, Peter, who is my brother and believes in my dreams. Clare and Roland Johnson added much insight to this endeavor. Kevin Summers and Carol Croake are my two Middletown guardian angels, and their faith renewed my enthusiasm. How fortunate I am to write for the grand gentleman at the *Middletown Journal*, my pal and editor, Rick McCrabb. And Rick, thanks for the photos. Again the Haleys, Ken and Marilyn, were kind enough to let me be photographed in their lovely antique home by the talented Glenn and Melinda Hartong. During choppy times, Grace K. Hill, and Debbie and Cliff Radel have motivated me to continue my dreams. Three cheers to the caring people at the historic homes for sharing pictures of their historic sites in this book. And Bravo to the managers of the shows whose photos presented throughout my writing help convey the joy of antiquing. One lady is my hero of heroes. According to the head of WVXU, Dr. James C. King, she single-handedly got me my NPR radio show, *Keep Antiquing!* Not only did Lee Hay do that, but she even proofread this manuscript along with our mutual friend, Margie Hays. Thanks to a very dear lady who shall remain nameless but I will give her initials... C. P. H. My sister, Debbie Bigelow, and her wonderful husband, Ron, were my colleagues who helped deliver an antique wedding present that has given joy to its recipients and to me for being able to share the adventure with you. My life has been blessed by two exceptional relatives. I never stop missing them. My antiquer Aunt Panny (Frances Loomis Wilson) has guided me to becoming a loving uncle and a successful antiquer. If it weren't for the most devoted grandmother, Frances LaRocque Lennon, I would not even be here today. My Gram not only taught me to be a gentleman, but she gave me my first antique. Her devotion and love warms me to this very day. And applause to my acquisitions editor at Krause Publications, Paul Kennedy, for going out on an (antiques) limb for me. And finally, I want to say *merci beaucoup* to Dan Brownell, who edited this book with expertise and sensitivity towards its appreciative author.

PART I

BECOMING A BELIEVER

1

You Really CAN Afford Antiques!

HELP IS ON THE WAY

Have you been flirting with antiques, but been hesitant to commit to a relationship? Do you gasp with horror at the astronomical prices quoted on antique shows? Have you decided not to become a collector because you're afraid of being snookered? If so, you're not alone! With the cost of trendy, museum-quality pieces skyrocketing, many of you are complaining, "I love antiques, but I can't afford them!" My response to your frustration: relax.

. . . .

Do you gasp with horror at the price of antiques? Relax! I'm about to show you how you really CAN afford them.

. . . .

Although you may think your dreams are futile, you really CAN afford antiques. As your frugal antiques coach, I'll explain how you can buy beautiful pieces without drowning in debt. I'll teach you practical and fun techniques to purchase inexpensive, first-class antiques and semi-antiques/collectibles. In essence, I am going to show you how to shop for champagne-quality items on a beer budget. All types of antiques—furniture, china, glass, pewter, textiles, and paint-ings—will soon be within your reach.

How is this possible? First, I'm going to change your mis-conceptions about antiques; in doing so, I'll free you from the limitations you've placed on yourself. You will soon know all the secrets to affordable antiques—what to look for and what to avoid, the best time to shop for antiques, and how to negotiate.

As for your concerns about being taken for a ride, fear not. I've outlined tips for safe shopping and included antiques price ceilings (to be explained later.) My goal is to help you gain the expertise you need to shop with confidence while staying within a reasonable budget.

. . . .

You will soon know all the secrets to affordable antiques—what to look for and what to avoid, the best time to shop for antiques, and how to negotiate.

. . . .

Most importantly, you'll bring home the antiques of your dreams—beautiful pieces that will enrich your life with lasting delight.

To date, scores of books have been written about antiques, but this one is unique. I know because I've been reading or thumbing through so many through the years. Some antique books focus on museum-quality pieces that are photogenic but extremely costly. Although these upscale albums adorn many coffee tables, they have a serious drawback.

NO $50,000 ANTIQUES HERE

Those gorgeous publications that claim that prime spot in front of the sofa could be downright disheartening to most of us because few of them actually focus on the needs of the everyday collector. So before we go any further, I want you to know that this primer is no coffee-table book. That means you won't find information about a $50,000 chair that once belonged to the Duchess of Somewhere. Instead, this collector-friendly manual is packed with insights that will make you a successful collector on a shoestring.

Ways will be revealed to get the look of $50,000 antiques (such as this glorious highboy) at a fraction of this price.

(Photo courtesy of Skinner's Auction Company)

Also, never forget that for every antique that's worth a fortune, thousands of others are available at very reasonable prices. Television shows featuring antiques may make it seem that all antiques are expensive, but that's because the costliest items get the most attention when the cameras are rolling. Believe me, I know what I am talking about because I have appraised for the *Antiques Roadshow*.

YOUR ANTIQUE COACH'S CREDENTIALS

Antiques are indeed a sport. Just look at these late-1800s photos of an athlete at Brady's Gymnasium in Washington, D.C.
(Photo courtesy of Skinner's Auction Company of Boston)

My whole life revolves around antiques—always has, always will. When other guys were playing baseball, I was trekking to farm auctions with my antiquer Aunt Panny. It never occurred to me that I was missing out on sports because I have always regarded antiquing as a game. Antiquing, like athletics, is a happy pastime that involves exercise, practice, timing, and sometimes even proper attire. Although scouting for antiques at shows may not seem as strenuous as playing football or tennis, it is nonetheless a physical activity benefiting both the body and mind.

As an adult, my passion for antiques took over my life. After graduate school, I opened a small antiques shop, which I operated for a few years. For over twenty-five years, I have been a full-time, independent appraiser of antiques. And along the way, I've written books and newspaper columns, had my own television and radio shows, and frequently been invited to speaking engagements. In addition, I teach antiques classes at the University of Cincinnati.

My broad background allows me to present a knowledgeable and unbiased perspective from various points of view— dealer, appraiser, collector, writer, instructor, and television and radio host. This varied and hands-on experience makes me a most trustworthy coach for both the beginner and the seasoned antiquer hungering for even more successful collecting. But I'm still a penny pincher at heart, and I would like to share my tight-fisted strategies with you.

What Are Loomisms?

Loomisms are maxims I've developed over a lifetime of experience with antiques. I like to keep them concise so they're memorable enough for you to recall as you stroll down the aisles at antique shows. You'll find these sayings sprinkled strategically throughout this book. I trust you'll find them practical and handy.

There's no sense wasting valuable time when there are so many affordable antiques beckoning to us, so let's get right to it. Soon you'll be convinced that you really CAN afford antiques. With that in mind, here's your first Loomism.

LOOMISM

Antiques are far less costly than you ever thought possible.

An Antique Dining Room Set Can Cost Less Than A 65-Inch Television?

In case you're skeptical about this statement, I thought I would show you an example to prove my point. I spent a delightful afternoon choosing antiques just for you. I was so pleased with the result that I had the room photographed for your own chairside tour.

This dining room setting is far more affordable than you ever dreamed.

(Photo courtesy of Middletown Journal)

I chose my examples carefully, as not just any would do. These antiques had to be good buys and handsome as well as practical. I began this fun adventure at one of my favorite middle-priced emporiums, the Middletown Antiques Mall in Middletown, Ohio. With help from my friends—owner Carol Croake and dealer Don Havens—we created a setting that emulates those you see in swanky stores like Bloomingdale's

· ·

When I reveal the total cost of this room,
you'll be amazed at how inexpensive antiques
can be. The catch, though, is that you
have to use my techniques.

· ·

and Marshall Field's. Our collection achieved a major breakthrough, however. Not only is this display completely decorated with authentic antiques and semi-antiques/collectibles, but it's affordable to boot. When I reveal the total cost of this room, you'll be amazed at how inexpensive antiques can be. The catch, though, is that you have to use my techniques.

A VINTAGE 1930S ROOM

Take a good look at our vintage 1930s display room. The dining suite is crafted of walnut, a timeless and ever-popular wood you'll learn more about in Chapter 6. The style was the pinnacle of fashion for furniture in the late 1500s during the reign of Queen Elizabeth I of England. The design was dubbed "Tudor" in honor of her last name. And now, in the new millennium, these 1930s Tudor-style pieces are highly esteemed by collectors.

* * *

Tudor furniture was the pinnacle of fashion in the late 1500s. And now, 1930s Tudor-style furniture is highly esteemed by collectors.

* * *

The china closet displays a beautiful set of Japanese Noritake china. During the Great Depression, brides really adored this brand, and new sets by this famous maker continue to be a favorite wedding present.

The table is large enough to seat six people comfortably. However, the bad news for the seller (but oh-so-favorable for us) is that it no longer has its original leaves, which once greatly expanded its seating capacity. That so-called "defect" helped stretch our purchasing power. And besides, as you're cleaning up after your company, you'll probably realize that six chairs are plenty.

Note the matching armchair and side chair positioned at each end of the table. They're original to the set. Now check the other four chairs. You'll have to look very closely to see that although their backs are similar to the armchair and side

Our dining room even has an early 1900s rendition of this 1500s Brussels tapestry.

(Photo courtesy of Skinner's Auction Company)

chair, they aren't exact duplicates. Selecting a dining suite lacking a complete set of matching chairs is a shrewd buying strategy. How that really stretches your budget will be made clearer later when I explain the advantages of selecting odd chairs.

. . . .

Selecting a dining suite lacking a complete set of matching chairs is a shrewd buying strategy.

. . . .

The table is arranged for Thanksgiving dinner, a celebration that gives us the opportunity to use china, flatware, linens, and other mementos from bygone days. Notice the 1880s castor set with its various bottles for vinegar, oil, pepper, and other condiments used to spice up meals. Little details about antiques make collecting all the more enjoyable and show us how people lived in the past.

The candlesticks on the center of the table are Depression glass, a widely collected item from the economically troubled 1930s, which accounts for its name. The cloth napkins and the silver-plated knives and forks add old-time pizzazz.

Who wouldn't feel like nobility when using the hundred-year-old silver-plated tea service resting so regally on the buffet? Even the large sideboard, so roomy for storage, is part of this dining suite. And notice the world-famous white Wedgwood china bowl from England resting near the tea service.

Can you believe this room even has artwork? On the wall you'll find an original oil painting from the early 1900s. Perhaps you have seen tapestries such as ours near the picture, dating from the early 1900s, in your own local antiques shops. The clock on the mantel was made in the mid-1800s, the era when the United States was the world leader in the mass-production of timepieces.

Here's another bonus of our treasures. Not only are these keepsakes good looking, but they're practical as well. We usually think of antiques as priceless objects to be roped off or encased in glass, only to be admired from afar but never used. Here guests are encouraged to sit on the chairs, dine from the china, or sip a cool drink from the glasses. This just shows that beauty, value, and practicality go hand in hand.

TAKE OUT YOUR PENCILS, PLEASE

Now that you've finished your tour, you're about to take your first and only quiz. Please check the appropriate box next to your estimate of the total cost of this room.

- ☐ $2,000-$3,000
- ☐ $3,000-$4,000
- ☐ $4,000-$5,000
- ☐ $5,000-$6,000
- ☐ $6,000-$7,000

Before I reveal whether or not you passed this quiz, I want to tell you the secret of my success. The secrets to assembling this terrific room at a really affordable price followed my guidelines explained in this book. No one would claim that this display is worthy of *Architectural Digest* or that it is museum quality, but that's exactly what makes it so charming. Everything here is all very affordable. In fact, it was even more

* *

Not only are antiques good-looking,
but they're practical as well.
They should be used as well as admired.

* *

affordable than I expected.

The total cost of this room (before price negotiation and sales tax) is $152 less than the cost of a 65-inch, big-screen, stereo color television recently advertised by a national appliance store. This vintage 1930s room can be yours for $3,147 (and maybe less, after you've mastered the principles of price negotiation detailed in Chapter 7).

An itemized list follows to help you fully grasp how afford-able these and so many other antiques and semi-antiques/col-lectibles really are.

RETAIL PRICES FOR THE
VINTAGE 1930S DINING ROOM

Item	Approximate age (in years)	Price
Dining suite	70	$1,150
(table, two chairs, buffet, china closet)		
Four dining chairs	50	$250
Knives and forks for six	70-80	$28
Noritake china		
from Japan for eight	70-80	$350
Six napkins	50-60	$6
Wedgwood china bowl	60	$125
Condiment/castor set	120	$75
Pair of candlesticks	70	$35
Tea service	100	$250
Bust of lady	80	$85
Twelve water goblets	50	$40
Glass dinner bell	50	$5
Clock	150	$185
Painting	80	$250
Six glass dessert plates	65	$48
Glass bowl	110	$25
Wine holder	50-60	$65
French tapestry	100	$175
Grand Total:		$3,147

Get a good look at this very reasonably priced maple set.

(Photo courtesy of Middletown Journal*)*

GOING THE EXTRA MILE

Maybe I should rest my case about the affordability of antiques. However, I feel it is important enough a topic for me to try to totally convince you. While shopping for that 1930s dining room suite, I also stumbled on a delightful dinette set from the 1940s. This little beauty was a steal at $295. Obviously, someone else agreed with me because it had been sold just before I spotted it. As they say, "All's fair in love and antiquing."

A LATE 1940s SETTING

Take a close look at the photo of this charming, late 1940s dinette suite. Wouldn't it look grand in the corner of any kitchen? It's made of solid maple in the ever-popular "Early American" style based on furniture designs of the 1700s. It includes a dining table with a center leaf, two side drop-leaves, four chairs, and a hutch. The setting features two coffee mills, napkins, milk-glass candlesticks, martini glasses, and Japanese china. This set, which delighted me as well as the lucky buyer, is a great example of a semi-antique/collectible. I'll talk more about this category of antiques, so brimming with bargains, in Chapter 3.

CAN YOU BELIEVE IT COSTS LESS THAN A WASHER AND DRYER?

If you thought the price of the 1930s room was surprising, then you'll be astonished at this one. Just imagine that even in

. . . .

Just imagine that even in the twenty-first century, a room can be furnished with antiques and semi-antiques/ collectibles for less than the cost of a washer and dryer.

. . . .

the twenty-first century, a room can be furnished with antiques and semi-antiques/collectibles for less than the cost of a washer and dryer. Isn't it amazing that the dinette set plus furnishings cost $154 less than a Frigidaire Crown Series washing machine and dryer set advertised by a national appliance store?

As impossible as it seems, this room setting cost only $846. The display with its incredible prices demonstrates that sometimes bargaining isn't necessary. (Those special cases are explained in chapter 7.) Following is the list of the items, with age and retail price, to show you how affordable these items really are.

⌒

Retail Prices for the Vintage 1940s Dining Area

Item	Approximate age (in years)	Price
Dinette set, (hutch, table, six chairs)	50-60	$295
Eight napkins	50	$15
Coffeepot	100	$55
Milk glass candlesticks	100	$35
Basket	40	$35
Pair of candlesticks	60	$30
Glass sugar bowl and creamer	50	$15
Silver-plated knife and spoon	60	$6
Glass ashtray	30	$2
Four martini glasses	50	$8
China from Japan for twelve	40-50	$185
Eight water goblets	40-50	$80
Coffee mill	30	$65
Second coffee mill	50	$20
Grand Total:		$846

I hope you agree that the first model room, and especially this second beauty, proves my first Loomism: "Antiques are far

. . . .

So understand right now that you no longer have to just dream about the antiques you've been craving because they are about to be yours.

. . . .

less costly than you ever thought possible." So understand right now that you no longer have to just dream about the antiques you've been craving because they are about to be yours. And this is just the beginning! Later, you'll master a great deal more—from buying antiques for less than a dollar (there are plenty) to getting that once-in-a-lifetime, oh-so-special antique.

Buying Champagne Antiques on a Beer Budget

How Your Antiques Coach Became a Believer

I hope you're euphoric now that you know you really CAN afford antiques. But before I reveal savvy techniques for finding antiques at unheard-of figures, I want to tell you how I learned to buy top quality antiques at bargain basement prices.

When I was a little boy, my father said, "The trouble with you, Frankie, is that you have champagne taste on a beer budget." Until a few years ago, that was the unspectacular story of my life. But that changed when I adopted a new attitude that helped me acquire a Dom Perignon antique at a Budweiser price.

Most of us have at least one possession that we've yearned for our entire lives. In my case, I felt I really didn't need any more antiques—except one. Ever since I visited the Joseph Loomis homestead in East Windsor, Connecticut, I had hankered for a certain type. While touring my ancestral home, parts of which date to 1638, I stumbled upon "it," and that stunner took my breath away. In one of the rooms of the white saltbox house, I found a cherry Queen Anne highboy. This gem from the 1700s was a tall chest of drawers resting on curvy cabriole legs. From that day on, I dreamed of having a treasure like Grandpa Joe's, but it seemed impossible because it cost far more than I could afford.

That changed after I learned some shrewd moves. Never doubt that know-how can produce wonders. Oddly enough, I miraculously acquired the antique of my dreams during a very scary time in my life when I was battling a severe medical problem. I was suffering from a hernia that required a second operation. Unfortunately, I had complications. A hematoma gave my stomach a bow shape that looks great on a 1790s half-round table, but not on me. For two weeks, the dressings from my surgery had to be changed hourly. Forgive me for sharing these gory details, but I want you to know how terrified I was so you can fully appreciate the positive power of antiques.

Several weeks after leaving the hospital, I attended a splendid antiques show called Heartland in Richmond, Indiana. Considering my illness, it was a bigger treat than ever to attend that year. You see, antiquing is one of the great joys of my life. This wonderful pastime always helps me forget my troubles as I cruise aisle after aisle surveying antiques and reading their descriptions. That was just what I intended to do

. . . .

This wonderful pastime always helps me forget my troubles as I cruise aisle after aisle surveying antiques and reading their descriptions.

. . . .

(ever so sluggishly) with my walking pal and fellow antiquer, Pete. We spotted a few highboys and checked their prices. One mahogany beauty in super condition was marked $8,000. That highboy might as well have been priced a million dollars, since I had lost work time because of my condition. Unfortunately, the Loomis Antiques Fund was almost empty because I had missed work for some time. When you run your own business, there's no such thing as a paid sick day.

Hooray for Defects

As closing time approached, I spotted another highboy, and it was love at first sight! It knocked my socks off. No doubt about it, I had never seen a more stunning 1700s Queen Anne highboy. I liked it even better than the one at Grandpa Joe's. It wasn't delicate or dainty looking, which is typical of that style. It was robust with bowed, fat cabriole legs. And like me, it had scars and nicks. The marks are called "distressing" or "the kiss of time." They are the result of furniture being loved and used

· ·

Scars and marks are called "distressing" or the "kiss of time." They are the result of furniture being loved and used and make antiques look old in a distinguished way.

· ·

and make antiques look old in a distinguished way. (In Chapter 14, I'll elaborate on this trait and how it creates bargains.) For the time being, let me tell you how that highboy's less-than-perfect condition yielded a financial windfall.

The dealers were Tom and Darlene Brown from McMurray, Pennsylvania. Darlene was honest and pointed out the highboy's flaws. It was a "married piece," meaning the top and bottom sections were both old but had been taken from different highboys. So I learned that the beautiful piece charming me that day had a top and base that most likely had been mated within the last fifty years.

LOOMISM

A no-longer-mint, yet quality antique can often be purchased for much less money than if it were still perfect.

Then the dealers mentioned another defect—its replaced handles. The blemishes on that highboy were drawbacks to upscale collectors who wanted perfect antiques, but not to me. The so-called blemishes made the highboy more alluring because they reduced its price and brought it into my range. Then and there, I decided the way to achieve my cham-

pagne dreams on my beer budget was to buy what others considered marred. To me, that dazzling highboy seemed worthy of the finest museum and most definitely deserving to hold my shorts and socks.

Things got even better when Darlene's price became even friendlier. She explained it was the end of the show, and they didn't want to haul the highboy home. (Chapter 10 discusses the advantage of arriving late at exhibitions to get great prices.) Then Tom said he would take another $100 off, arriving at the final figure of $3,400. This was 50 to 75 percent less than the price would have been if the highboy had been in perfect condition. A gentleman's handshake closed the deal. I put $500 down and gave my word to pay the balance within sixty days.

The following Monday turned out to be a really rough day. That afternoon I met my surgeon at the emergency room to restitch my incision to stop the bleeding. As my doctor was repairing me, I reminisced about the Queen Anne highboy I had thought I couldn't possibly afford. The reverie brought me great joy during a very stressful situation. I am happy to tell you that the highboy still brings me great pleasure every second of every day.

Is any of this antique silver in less than pristine condition? Only your auctioneer knows for sure.

(Photo courtesy of Garth's Auctions, Inc.)

LOOMISM

The defects in an antique that seem so serious when shopping appear to fade once they're in your home.

Is this 1790 English pitcher any less beautiful because it is damaged? For us, it is more desirable because its less-than-perfect state makes it more affordable.

(Photo courtesy of Skinner's Auction Company)

When my highboy was moved into my room, my joy grew even greater because something magical happened. The defects that the Browns pointed out seemed to vanish once it was in place. The highboy still looks superb in front of the salmon-colored wallpaper that brings out the auburn tones of the cherry wood. Truthfully, only an expert could spot its flaws.

LOOMISM

Antiques affirm the joy of living.

When King Francois I of France brought Leonardo da Vinci's painting the "Mona Lisa" from Italy to his palace Fontainebleau near Paris, he probably wasn't any more thrilled with it than I was with my highboy. Moreover, when the morning sun flooded my eighteenth-century treasure, I

knew things would get better. The highboy—the antique of my dreams that I always felt was beyond my wallet—was proof. Looking back on those trying days, it's clear that event marked the beginning of my physical and mental renaissance. So now you know the most meaningful reason to collect antiques—the joy they bring to life.

Again, my regrets for this gruesome story, but I want you to fully relish the miraculous way this piece lifted my spirits. Rest assured that antiques can have the same glorious effect on you, too. That's the great power of antiques!

You're on your way to antiques paradise because you've already learned two important truths: first, you'll be able to afford antiques, and second, they'll bring you great happiness. With a little tutoring, you'll be able to reach your goals. Whether you're a freshman or post-graduate antiquer, great times are ahead.

The shrewd buyer of these late 1800s tables got the 1700s look without paying a museum quality price.

(Photo courtesy of Skinner's Auction Company)

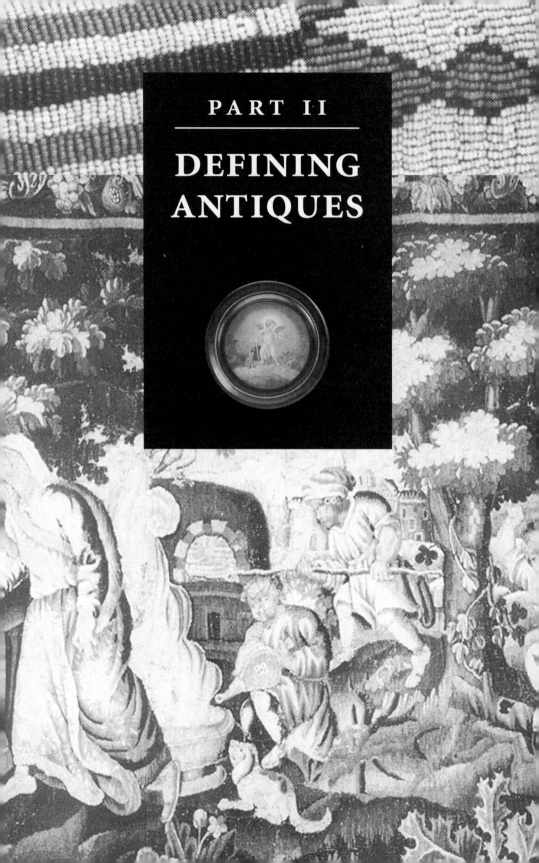

PART II
DEFINING ANTIQUES

3

Do They Still Make Antiques?

THE TERM "ANTIQUE" DEFINED

Your first step towards acquiring affordable antiques is to familiarize yourself with collecting terminology. Even though the definition of "antique" can be as confusing and intimidating as trying to decipher a cell phone manual, you have nothing to fear because your antiques coach will demystify all the perplexing twaddle for you. Clarifying and simplifying the definition of "antique" will give you a strong footing for successful and snookering-free shopping.

. . . .

Clarifying and simplifying the definition of "antique" will give you a strong footing for successful and snookering-free shopping.

. . . .

THE ANTIQUE MEANING OF "ANTIQUES"

Before the 1800s, the term "antique" referred to artifacts from ancient times crafted by the Greeks, Romans, or Egyptians. Today, auction houses like Sotheby's and Skinner's use the word "antiquities" to describe relics from those ancient civilizations.

CURIOS

As collecting became more popular in the 1800s, the meaning of the term "antique" began changing. Artifacts from ancient civilizations were still called antiques, but items from the more recent past, such as the 1600s and 1700s, were labeled "curios." This explains why author Charles Dickens chose the name, *The Old Curiosity Shop,* for his 1840 best-selling novel about Nell Trent and her grandfather, who owned a second-hand store.

In the Victorian era, the curio cabinet, a piece of furniture previously considered essential only for museums, became mainstream in homes. Curio cabinets graced many parlors, displaying various collections.

A vintage 1905 postcard depicting "The Old Curiosity Shop" in London, England, which in today's terminology means antiques shop.

(Photo courtesy of Karen Plunkett Powell)

By 1890, the term "antique" was not only applied to artifacts from the ancient world, but to all things that were considered old. If Mr. Dickens had written his book in the early twentieth century, he might have named it *The Antiques Shop* instead. By then the term "antique" had become more commonplace than the word "curio." Thankfully, that charming and archaic name, "curio cabinet," has stuck to this day because the term "antique cabinet" has an entirely different meaning, as you are discovering.

THE ELITIST DEFINITION OF "ANTIQUE"

By 1900, so many Americans were buying, selling, and collecting antiques that standards were needed. Consequently, an early doctrine emerged declaring that genuine antiques must be made before 1820. According to most historians, by that year the Industrial Revolution was in full swing. This milestone marked a turning point; most household goods were then machine made rather than handcrafted. Thus, to qualify as a genuine antique, an object had to have been handmade before 1820. I call this doctrine the "Elitist Rule."

TWO REASONS TO IGNORE THE ELITIST RULE

1. The edict is too restrictive because, in general, the majority of antiques made before 1820 are outrageously priced. However, in future chapters, I'll show you some ways to acquire superb pre-1820 antiques at bargain prices.
2. If celestial prices aren't enough to steer you away from the 1820 rule, consider the following fact. Being old or handmade does not guarantee quality. Always remember that quality is far more important than age. Just because a piece was made before 1820 doesn't mean it's first-class. An item could have been "low end" from the very beginning.

A Native American beaded-hide knife sheath made by the Sioux around 1880 is a fine example of an antique.

(Photo courtesy of Skinner's Auction Company)

Uncle Sam's Definition of "Antique"

Collecting became even more stylish in the early 1900s. Not surprisingly, the United States government became involved by defining the term "antique." When American tourists brought antiques into this country, they had to pay duty, a tax devised to protect homegrown industries. But officials soon realized that these artifacts benefited our culture, so Uncle Sam created a more liberal ruling. The U.S. Customs Office declared that if an item was a hundred or more years old, it was an antique and could enter the country duty free.

Early 1900s items such as this music box have matured into genuine antiques.

(Photo courtesy of Skinner's Auction Company)

THE FIRST ANTIQUES FROM THE TWENTIETH CENTURY, COURTESY OF UNCLE SAM

The definition of antique according to customs laws is subject to update annually. Such an adaptable and practical approach allows more items to qualify each year as genuine antiques, keeping supplies available and prices under control.

The new millennium ushered in more than a new century—it heralded an exciting era for American collectors. For the first time in history, we can call goods from the early years of the twentieth century genuine antiques. Thanks to Uncle Sam, Victrolas and 1903 oak dining tables with big hairy animal claw feet are the "real McCoy."

Paintings are also antiques. These oil portraits of an African American gentleman and lady were captured by an informally trained artist about 1893.

(Photo courtesy of Skinner's Auction Company)

Africa has fine antiques, including this late 1800s wooden headrest.

(Photo courtesy of Skinner's Auction Company)

The ever-changing definition for antiques constantly reminds us that what seems old to one may appear newish to another. These highly desirable 1965 wire chairs are a good example of this principle.

(Photo courtesy of Skinner's Auction Company)

THE AMERICAN INTERPRETATION OF "ANTIQUE"

Antiques are an even a bigger craze now than they were in the early 1900s. Ever notice the numerous antiques shops nestled in downtown areas or the numerous antiques malls sprouting along expressways? Even with Uncle Sam's ever expanding ruling, the collecting fervor diminishes the stock of antiques. Therefore, we need a slightly revised unofficial definition to ensure a constant supply of antiques. To keep reserves bountiful, which also helps hold prices in line, brand anything made before 1920 as antique.

This date isn't arbitrary, but for the present it makes sense because that year designates a real cultural and historic shift. World War I ended most old-fashioned ways, and our high-

. . . .

The year 1920 is significant because it designates a real cultural and historic shift.

. . . .

tech lifestyle began in the 1920s. That eternally modern decade witnessed the construction of the Chrysler Building in New York City, Lindbergh flying non-stop to Paris, knee-

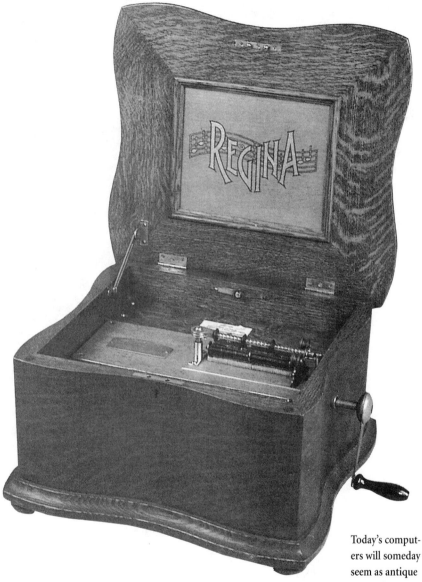

length dresses replacing long trailing ones, and automobiles becoming almost as universal then as television is now.

So keep in mind that our geographical origin also affects our perception of antiques. On the East Coast of North America, the earliest non-Native American antiques date to

Today's computers will someday seem as antique to our descendants as this early 1900s Regina music box seems to us.

(Photo courtesy of Skinner's Auction Company)

This circa 1900 sheet-music cabinet is a genuine antique according to Uncle Sam, and the punch bowl is a genuine antique according to my Loomism.

(Photo courtesy of Middletown Journal)

the arrival of Europeans. And rest assured that this date works very well for the majority of East Coast collectors, too. Thus, pre-1820 antiques can be more prevalent in cities like New York, Boston, and Charleston than in the rest of the country. Because much of the rest of America was settled later, my 1920 guideline makes sense for most American and Canadian collectors. The majority of Europeans, however, have a very different opinion on the matter.

LOOMISM

Consider anything made before 1920 as antique.

THE EUROPEAN INTERPRETATION OF "ANTIQUE"

The European viewpoint really illustrates how location affects the definition of "old." I learned a lot while in France, which is as much a magnet to antiquers as Rome is to Roman Catholics and Florida is to "snowbirds." My recent visits in France have given me a whole different perspective about the subject.

A few years ago, I was fortunate enough to visit the beautiful city of Avignon in the south of France. The most popular tourist spot in that town is the Pope's palace, constructed in stages between 1309 and 1376. During those turbulent years for ecclesiastics, the Pope and his court ruled the Roman Catholic Church from there, rather than from its former (and later reinstated) headquarters in Rome.

- -

Europeans have a different perception of "old" because their history goes back so much further than ours.

- -

As I toured the huge, historic site, I realized that this museum was a real lesson to us American antiquers about our standards concerning antiques. I stated that we in the United States can consider something antique if it dates before the 1920s. France and the rest of Europe would probably get a chuckle from my interpretation, which works so well for most North Americans. Obviously, Europeans have a different perception because their history goes back so much further than ours.

Looking at the various religious artifacts in Avignon, it occurred to me that we Americans think Versailles, the palace built by Louis XIV outside of Paris, France, is really old, but compared to the Pope's palace, it seems pretty recent. The Papal residence was about three hundred years old in 1661 when King Louis started work on his chateau.

European antiques tend to be older and often date from the 1600s or early 1700s.

(Photo courtesy of Skinner's Auction Company)

My observations concerning antiques advanced the following year when I returned to France and sojourned in the dazzling city of Nimes. Located near Avignon, it is justly called "the French Rome," because the Romans built fine edifices there during the time of Christ. That is the era for "antiquities," which, as I previously explained, is the name given to objects dating from Classical times.

Two Roman relics—the temple, known as the "Maison Carree" (Rectangular Building), and the arena—taught me

. . . .

While visiting these sites, I decided that the Pontiff's "cottage" in Avignon seemed practically modern compared to the Nimes edifices, which are more than a millennium older.

. . . .

Talk about old! These Pre-Columbian pottery figurines from South America date from 1,000-2,000 B.C.

(Photo courtesy of Skinner's Auction Company)

more about the ever-evolving definition of antiques. These monuments dating from about 20 A.D. are literally antiques according to the original definition of the term. They testify to the marvels of Roman technology because the arena, resembling Rome's Colosseum, is used for rock concerts, and the temple is a functioning museum. While visiting these sites, I decided that the Pontiff's "cottage" in Avignon seemed practically modern compared to the Nimes edifices, which are more than a millennium older.

Other examples of really old antiques are these figurines from China dating from 202 B.C. to 920 A.D.

(Photo courtesy of Skinner's Auction Company)

I thought nothing could surpass those Roman master-pieces for age, but was I ever mistaken. Recently, I went back to Nimes with my friends Dianne and Pete and visited its archaeological museum. Enclosed in a glass case was an astonishing relic that shed even more light on the issue about the age of antiques. The artifact was an earthenware jar dating

. . . .

My travels in France have taught me that
"antique is in the eye of the beholder."
What one culture thinks is old,
another considers relatively new.

. . . .

from 1,500 to 1,800 B.C. Astonishingly, that ceramic piece was well over a thousand years old when the Romans were building their structures in Nimes. Suddenly, the amphitheater and the temple seemed modern, and the Pope's palace practically high-tech compared to the jar.

My travels in France have taught me that "antique is in the eye of the beholder." What one culture thinks is old, another considers relatively new. Maybe modern Egyptians and Greeks grin when they hear Europeans talking about what they consider antique.

Let's return to our side of the Atlantic and the North American perspective towards antiques. Keep my 1920 date as your cut-off for genuine antiques and you'll succeed handsomely.

SEMI-ANTIQUES/COLLECTIBLES

Since a major part of collecting these days involves items dating from the late twentieth century, we need to focus on those pieces. In addition, it's fascinating to observe how the definition of antique has a direct relationship to one's birth date. For example, the blond furniture from the 1950s originally

A circa 1960
television seems
newish to a baby
boomer, but
ancient to the
computer
generation.

*(Photo courtesy of
Skinner's Auction
Company)*

known as Swedish Modern, has been revived with that trendy
Retro designation. Antique malls are full of Retro pieces that
were originally sold in the 1950s or 1960s at stores all across
America. To the computer generation born in the 1970s, these

. . . .

*To the computer generation born in the 1970s,
Retro seems as ancient as claw-foot bathtubs
do to baby boomers.*

. . . .

Here is another formerly high-tech item that now falls under the heading of "Retro."
(Photo courtesy of Skinner's Auction Company)

This Eames lounge chair and ottoman first manufactured by Herman Miller in 1956 are prime examples of "Retro."
(Photo courtesy of Skinner's Auction Company)

A 1963 walnut desk has that streamlined Art Deco look that "Retro" collectors love.
(Photo courtesy of Skinner's Auction Company)

pieces seem as ancient and as fashionable as claw-foot bath-tubs do to baby boomers.

These interpretations of the term "antique" and the term "Retro" remind me of how different my perspective was from my grandmother's. Those Retro pieces are to me what 1920s furniture were to her. When I was a teen collector showing her what I considered a treasure, she exclaimed, "What do you want that for? I threw one out just like it forty years ago."

1970s Wedgwood china falls under the heading of "semi-antique/ collectible."

(Photo courtesy of Skinner's Auction Company)

This 1940s mahogany secretary/desk duplicates the look of 1700s pieces at a far more affordable price.

(Photo courtesy of Middletown Journal*)*

Now in this century, I refuse to say something like that to my nephew. When Ryan shows me a less-than-ancient memento, Uncle Frank replies with a chuckle, "Retro is awesome." Your antiques coach prudently leaves the answer to the question, "Is it junk or antique?" up to you.

So what do we label the Retro items from the *I Love Lucy*, *The Brady Bunch*, and the *Mary Tyler Moore Show* decades? Because they're maturing, I call them semi-antiques/collectibles. Over time, this label will need updating, as these wonderful semi-antiques/collectibles will eventually become genuine antiques.

A charming semi-antique/collectible is this Kodak 1939 New York World's Fair "Bullet" camera.

(Photo courtesy of Skinner's Auction Company)

SEMI-ANTIQUE/COLLECTIBLES OFFER BARGAINS

Although semi-antiques/collectibles lack the status of genuine antiques, they are just as well made as their ancestors. But their youth makes them more enticingly affordable. In time, this gang will cost much more after they have matured into authentic antiques.

· ·

Although semi-antiques/collectibles lack the status of genuine antiques, they are just as well made as their ancestors. But their youth makes them more enticingly affordable.

· ·

FUTURE ANTIQUES

After a lecture, a gentleman once asked me, "Do they still make antiques?" Believe it or not, until then, the thought had never occurred to me. His marvelous question helped me realize that, thankfully, antiques are still being made. Yes, they still make antiques, and thanks to the ever-evolving definition, new generations will have their share. In the twenty-second century, antiques will include quality items being created today, such as handmade quilts and hooked rugs.

Antiques Have Many Perks

WHAT NAPOLEON MISSED

Now that the terms "antique" and "semi-antique/collectible" have been defined, it seems only natural for me to present you the many advantages they bring to our lives.

No doubt Napoleon rarely smiled—he was a nonantiquer.

(Photo courtesy of Skinner's Auction Company of Boston)

Legend records an account of a sovereign who really goofed when he turned down an opportunity to acquire an exquisite French cabinet. If this famous non-collector found out who now owns this masterpiece, he would turn over in his regal tomb at the Hotel des Invalides in Paris. Napoleon I, Emperor of France from 1804 to 1815, was offered a sumptuous cabinet that once belonged to in-laws of Queen Marie Antoinette of France. Bonaparte, who had little appreciation for peace and even less for curios, haughtily declared, "His majesty wants the new and not to buy old." What perks do antiques offer that Napoleon so thoughtlessly disregarded? The benefits fall into four main categories: practical, financial, intellectual, and emotional.

This oil painting by Walter Gay, (U.S.A., 1856-1937) really brings to life a 1700s French Louis XV and XVI interior.

(Photo courtesy of Skinner's Auction Company)

PRACTICAL PERKS
Mother Nature Loves Antiques

Remember how Gram critiqued my antique choices? Her remark, "I threw one out just like it forty years ago," suggests a rarely mentioned dividend of antiquing. Collecting is really a long-established form of recycling, which benefits our environment. Reusing discarded objects decreases the amount of trash entering landfills, and reclaiming wooden furniture saves trees by reducing demand for new wood.

. . . .

Collecting antiques is really a form of recycling, which benefits our environment. Reusing discarded objects decreases the amount of trash entering landfills, and reclaiming furniture saves trees by reducing demand for new wood.

. . . .

The adaptability of antiques is endless. Televisions and VCRs are probably the number one reason for the popularity of armoires.

(Photo courtesy of Middletown Journal*)*

No Assembly Required

A while back I wanted to become more high tech, so I bought a new computer desk for my office. (My emotional choice, an antique model, seemed impractical for this purpose.) I gave up

. . . .

Another benefit of antiques is that,
unlike most new furniture,
they don't require assembly.

. . . .

a postcard-perfect fall weekend to unpack the desk and put it together. This tedious job illustrated another gratifying aspect of collecting: antiques, unlike most new furniture or practically anything else for our homes, don't require assembly.

My grandmother had a dining suite similar to this Heywood Wakefield buffet from 1954, which today is called "Retro."

(Photo courtesy of Skinner's Auction Company)

FINANCIAL PERKS
Antiques Give More Dash for Your Cash

Not long ago, my family visited an outdoor show in Allegan, Michigan. A 1940s end table flirted with my sister, Debbie. It

ended up in her family's living room for only $40. My nephew, Ryan, took home a 1915 oak rocking chair for a mere $30.

It might seem unbelievable that in the twenty-first century you can buy a rocking chair and table for under $100, but it's true. Although these pieces aren't museum caliber, they are well made and charming. In contrast, what can you buy new for $70 in a furniture store (or even at Target)? You can actually buy better quality furniture for less by shopping for antiques.

This 1744 cabinet, which retailed for $850 in 1937, has maintained its value and could easily go at auction today for $6,000 to $8,000.

(Photo courtesy of Antiques Magazine)

Antiques Retain Value Better Than New

The instant your new item leaves the store, it's considered used merchandise and, therefore, plummets in value. Have you been to a garage sale where a downtrodden soul was trying to peddle a six-month old sofa? That demoralized individual might have been your antiques coach. After a day of wheeling and dealing on my driveway, I was thrilled to get $65 for what originally cost $650. That experience taught me that antiques are far better investments when compared to new items.

Antiques May Increase In Value

Unlike my former sofa, antiques keep their value and sometimes increase. If you compare prices from the past to current

This 1800s cupboard cleverly fits into a very narrow space in the dining room of the Centre family dwelling in the Shaker religious community of Shaker Village, Kentucky.

(Photo courtesy of Shaker Village of Pleasant Hill, Kentucky)

The same spot with the doors opened from hall to dining room. Pretty ingenious! The cupboard is made from cherry, a favorite wood for Shaker pieces.

(Photo courtesy of Shaker Village of Pleasant Hill, Kentucky)

ones, you'll be startled to see how much they've increased. For instance, when I was in graduate school, I bought a 1930s china closet. The layaway plan made it possible to make week-

* *

Unlike mass-produced furniture, antiques keep their value and often appreciate.

* *

ly payments until I had paid the full $175. That semi-antique/collectible is now worth $900 to $1,800. If I were to sell it, I would get an excellent return for my $175 investment. Best of all, it still looks grand in my dining room.

Antiques Offer Higher Quality

It doesn't take long to learn that antiques are usually better made than their modern counterparts. Older houses, as you know, have plastered walls, while contemporary homes have drywall. This similar disparity in quality exists between antiques and new goods. Modern furniture highlights the craftsmanship found in antiques. Current furniture may have particleboard or cardboard backs, unlike the solid wood backs used in antiques. When modern furniture features "carving," it is usually plastic, not the painstakingly hand carved wood found in vintage pieces. Modern furniture is assembled with weak, ugly staples, rather than with glue and screws. The same contrast in quality is evident in other products, from china to silver. While some modern goods have quality construction, they are the exception and are very expensive. How many of us have checkbooks that can tackle their lofty prices?

INTELLECTUAL PERKS
Antiques Teach History

Antiques make great history teachers because they offer personal and interesting insights into the past. For example, have you ever wondered why some old-fashioned chairs have casters on their front legs? Before central heating, they made scooting over to a warm fireplace much easier. Information like this illuminates the lifestyles and customs of our ancestors.

EMOTIONAL PERKS
Antiques Provide Mini Vacations

Have you ever heard the song Judy Garland sings in the 1950 movie *Summer Stock*? The lyrics include the words, "Forget your troubles; come on, get happy...." I always add, "...by going antiquing." Rummaging aisle after aisle at malls, shows, or flea markets makes troubles and stress disappear as you

This 1910ish postcard of State and Madison Streets in downtown Chicago
reveals that rushing is nothing new.

(Author's collection)

These 1900 German porcelain plaques reveal the racier side of our ancestors.

(Photo courtesy of Skinner's Auction Company)

What insight antiques give us about the past! This elephant-shaped inkwell must have brought chuckles every time a pen was dipped into it.

(Photo courtesy of Skinner's Auction Company)

. . . .

Antiques are great history teachers because they give us fascinating insights into the lifestyles of our ancestors.

. . . .

This toy trolley shows us how many tourists arrived at the Chicago World's Fair of 1893.

(Photo courtesy of Skinner's Auction Company)

Here's another history lesson. What do you think the small chest of drawers in the door of the Manigault House holds? It hides something necessary before indoor plumbing.

(Photo courtesy of Charleston Museum)

Antique photographs teach us so much about the past.
(Photo courtesy of Middletown Journal)

search for that special antique. Or better yet, just enjoy being a tourist while sightseeing and reading descriptions, which incidentally is an easy way to study antiques (more about this later).

Antiques Promotes Bonding

Another benefit of antiquing is that anyone tagging along will probably become a lifelong friend. I fondly reminisce with my buddies Pete and Dianne about one of our best-ever antiques rendezvous in the French paradise known as the Parisian Flea Market. We have also grown to respect our different tastes and shopping styles. At shows, one of us is the meanderer while the other two are sprinters. Our diverse modes complement each other; Dianne has spotted gems the too-hurried guys missed.

Antiques can work the same magic with relatives. Antiquing has made my sister and me even better pals, and we often plan our summer get-togethers around outdoor shows.

Now her husband, Ron, and their son, Ryan, join us. We some-day hope to snag my niece, "Miss" Mackenzie, and her hus-band, Kris, into our collecting group. (More about my efforts with those two in Chapter 16, which gives strategies to help you convert someone into an antiquer.)

Antiques And Feng Shui

For centuries, the Chinese have followed Feng Shui, the art of arranging objects to promote positive energy in homes and businesses. The philosophy incorporates many principles, but one in particular especially pertains to us.

One of the tenets of Feng Shui is the importance of sur-rounding ourselves with possessions that bring happiness and harmony. Antiques do this superbly. It doesn't matter if yours are pedigreed or mixed breeds; the important thing is to pick what you love. Persian carpets, 1900 oak furniture, 1930s Depression glass, Beatles memorabilia, English china, and baseball cards all can work their mystical charm by bringing happiness to their owners.

. . . .

One of the tenets of Feng Shui is the importance of surrounding ourselves with possessions that bring happiness and harmony. Antiques do this superbly.

. . . .

Forgive me for being so upbeat, but if you're a collector, you understand. Or if you are about to plunge into antiques, then you'll soon discover why I'm so enthusiastic. Let me illus-trate with a story to demonstrate their magic. While I was helping with the *Antiques Roadshow* in Louisville, Kentucky, a lady vigilantly holding a pink teacup and saucer to be appraised taught me the meaning of Feng Shui. Grasping her treasure was no easy chore, for an illness had gnarled her hands. But her grin reflected her rapture as she chattered to me about her grandmother's china. Just sharing her joy with me seemed to erase her discomfort.

Remember my account about the antique of my dreams and how you will get one, too? Even now the highboy brings me the same Feng Shui magic that it did during those appalling times by constantly reminding me of the beauty in this world.

I can testify from experience that a glance at a beloved heirloom can give you a thrill. Perhaps grandma's china or a favorite uncle's chair gives you good vibes. Precious family

Just looking at this circa 1907-1918 carousel horse by Stein and Goldstein of Brooklyn, New York, brings a smile.

(Photo courtesy of Skinner's Auction Company)

mementos such as these can keep beloved relatives always in your heart and give you peaceful thoughts during rough times. Just looking at my English blue-and-white Wedgwood china plates (only $6.50 each) does that to me. They always make me say, "How I love those plates." (You see, Wedgwood is one of my passions.) Antiques lift my spirits and constantly comfort me. They did it for my Louisville hero at the *Antiques Roadshow*, and yours will do the same for you. That's Feng Shui in action!

This painting by Zedekiah Belknap (U.S.A. 1781-1858) of child with doll captures the wonders of collecting.

(Photo courtesy of Skinner's Auction Company)

Just imagine that while resting in your recently acquired 1900 rocking chair that you sense the happy times the chair has witnessed. The antique's positive feelings are now yours until it goes on to the next person. And hopefully you will add even more delight to your antique for future generations to enjoy.

Antiques And Pets Are The International Language Of Friendship

Have you ever been at a party where the bragging, hot political debates, or trivial jabber is just too much? Or worse, you're enduring dead silence? Then, miraculously, the gathering becomes blissfully noisy, full of giggling and happy banter. Why? Someone probably mentioned pets. Conversations about antiques create the same transformation. Strangers have become pals comparing shows, dealers, prices, and collections. Dogs, cats, and antiques bring out the best in people

. . . .

Dogs, cats, and antiques bring out the best in people and are part of the international language of friendship.

. . . .

and are part of the international language of friendship.

Now that you know all the perks antiques bring to our lives, you probably realize why few (if any) portraits of Napoleon ever depicted him smiling.

When the Emperor rejected the cabinet, he not only lost the opportunity to own a magnificent piece of furniture, but he also missed out on the bonuses that come with antiques. Furthermore, today a descendent of his archenemy, King George III, owns this crème de la crème antique. According to David Linley in his superb book, *Extraordinary Furniture*, this showpiece embellishes the private apartments of Queen Elizabeth II at Windsor Castle.

PART III

THE SENSUAL APPROACH

Using Your Senses to Identify the Real McCoy

A Hands-On Method

Now that you know all the perks that antiques bring to our lives, you're ready for the next step—becoming an antiques sleuth, a Sherlock Holmes of heirlooms. Your goal is to learn

. . . .

You're ready to become an antiques sleuth. By learning to use your senses, you will learn to spot valuable antiques overlooked by less alert collectors.

. . . .

how to detect valuables that have been overlooked by less alert collectors. The first drill will call on your senses. Your eyes, fingers, heart, and even your posterior are about to make evaluating antiques as simple as making a peanut butter sandwich.

The Sensual Approach to Learning

The Sensual Approach to Learning came about one day after I read the biography of my favorite artist, Pierre Auguste Renoir. This master, who graced the world from 1841 to 1919, captured in his art the beauty and joy of life that the French call *joie de vivre*. One of Renoir's most heralded creations, *On the Terrace*, a masterpiece depicting a mother and her daughter, reigns as showstopper at the Art Institute of Chicago.

Jean Renoir, in *Renoir, My Father*, recorded what the master wrote near the end of his life: "Someone gave a picture by one of the great masters to one of my friends, who was delighted to have an object of undisputed value. He showed it off to everyone. One day he came rushing in to see me. He was overcome with joy. He told me naively that he had never understood until that morning why the picture was beautiful. Until then, he had always followed the crowd in being impressed only by the signature. My friend had just become a sensualist."

Monsieur Renoir Knew Best

What did Monsieur Renoir mean by being a sensualist? Let's check with an expert—a thick, leatherbound 1907 edition of *Webster's International Dictionary* that has been my steadfast mentor through the years. (Incidentally, I picked up this copy with cover badly worn for $5 at a street sale.) Mr. Webster's editors define a sensualist as "one given to the indulgences of the senses as a means of happiness." Renoir's friend became a sensualist when he started cherishing the delight he received every time his eyes caressed the painting.

LOOMISM

The Sensual Approach to Learning will help you become intimately acquainted with antiques. Your eyes, fingers, heart, and even the cushy part of your anatomy will enlighten you.

Renoir himself expressed the inexplicable joy that comes from owning beautiful objects. The painter taught me that while it's pleasing to purchase things that may increase in price, their true value is that they are an investment in happiness. So cherish your beloved keepsakes not for the profit they might bring, but for the charm and zest they add to your life.

Thus, Pierre Renoir became my role model and inspiration for creating the Sensual Approach to Learning. Now, I can pass this technique along to help you develop your command

. . . .

Cherish your beloved antiques not for the profit
they might bring, but for the charm and zest
they add to your life.

. . . .

of antiques. It's so simple you can learn it practically by osmosis. This means that, unlike more formal schooling, there will be no outside reading assignments that include wordy texts about as comprehensible and exciting as assembly instructions for a barbecue grill.

THE SENSUAL APPROACH TO LEARNING IN ACTION
⸻⸻⸻⸻⸻⸻⸻⸻⸻⸻⸻⸻⸻⸻⸻⸻⸻ ᏅᎧ

PART ONE: WINDOW SHOP AND READ

To put the Sensual Approach into practice, visit upscale antiques establishments or attend posh antiques shows. Top-drawer dealers, whether at shows, malls, or shops, provide fascinating details about age, wood, history, origin, and style when trying to peddle their sumptuous goods.

Leave your checkbook at home when visiting these places. You won't be going to purchase but to engage in a hands-on learning experience. Come to think of it—leave your cell phone behind as well so you can really concentrate. Be prepared to take your time and, if necessary, bring your reading glasses to scan fascinating information.

While you're on this adventure, pretend you're in charge of a fine arts fund with assets that even a great museum would envy. This harmless game will keep you from being intimidated by the prices and will allow you to focus on learning. You'll be amazed how much knowledge you'll accumulate in a single visit.

Your Heart

Prepare yourself for the Sensual Approach to Learning by focusing on objects that whet your appetite. It's far easier to learn and retain information about antiques that stir your passions than about those that leave you lukewarm.

Your Eyes

Learning how to study antiques with your eyes is one of the most essential skills to develop. The following example shows how you can become savvier about antiques. Imagine that, as you surf a sales area, you discover a chair with lovely cabriole legs. You gaze with admiration at the beautiful detailed work. Now close your eyes to create a mental picture of the celebrated bowed legs first created in the early 1700s. You'll be surprised at how easily you'll be able to spot them again.

. . . .

We all have a natural desire to explore objects by touch. This is a crucial, and perhaps the most enjoyable, element of the Sensual Approach.

. . . .

Your Fingers

We all have a natural desire to explore objects by touch. This is a crucial, and perhaps the most enjoyable, element of the Sensual Approach. Just do so carefully because you don't want to pay for damaged goods. Touch, or rather caress, any antique you want to study. Your fingertips can reveal a great deal. In fact, after reading the item's description, close your eyes once more, but this time gently rub the object to get the full impression of its texture—dents, curves, hardness or softness, and other tactile qualities. Exploring antiques through touch

To learn about colorful Majolica from the 1800s, visit genuine pieces in shops and shows and then touch reproductions in department stores.

(Photo courtesy of Skinner's Auction Company)

has many benefits, but I have chosen two that best illustrate the potential education you can gain through your fingertips.

BALL-AND-CLAW CARVED FEET

Check descriptions or ask to see a vintage 1700s chair with ball-and-claw carved feet.

As the name suggests, this type of foot resembles a bird's claw holding a ball. Now close your eyes and allow your fingers to explore the feet, vigorously massaging the carvings. You'll be able to feel that the carving is three-dimensional and crafted from a solid piece of wood. These qualities are typical of handmade furniture of the 1700s. This experience will prepare you well for future antiquing expeditions. When you encounter modern ball-and-claw feet, you'll be able to recognize the flatter and duller sensations, indicating that the carv-

ing is glued on or made from several pieces of wood. These characteristics are indicative of more recent construction.

Hand Painted China

If you find a china bowl that claims to be hand painted, give it the finger test. Rub your fingers over the motifs to determine if they have a slight "nubbiness." Nubs or bumps are the result of thick paint, which reveals that the ornamentation has been applied by hand.

Even Your Posterior

That tender part of your physique is a better instructor about woods than most reference books could ever be. As you meander through shops or shows, scout descriptions for two chairs—one with a mahogany seat and one with pine. Forget the silly notion that antique chairs are only decorative objects

Rub your fingers ever so gently over the curvy cabriole leg of this circa 1770 table, and you will fully relish the detailing involved in hand-carving.

(Photo courtesy of Skinner's Auction Company)

This 1600s chair
does not pass the
posterior test,
which is why it is
not as valuable as
younger, more
comfortable
chairs.

*(Photo courtesy of
Skinner's Auction
Company)*

and should never be used for their original purpose. Go ahead and test them, but be warned that you will react very differently to each. Your hindquarters won't be fond of the mahogany beauty. In fact, this dense reddish wood is downright posterior unfriendly. However, when you try the pine seat, you'll know right away why pine is a favorite for chair seats. As I shall say again and again, always give the posterior test before purchasing chairs (whether new or old) so you get comfortable as well as good-looking ones.

PART TWO: VISIT MUSEUMS, CONSULT VINTAGE CATALOGUES, AND WATCH MOVIES

Museum hopping is another excellent way to learn more about antiques. You'll view extraordinary dazzlers that most of us (even in our Technicolor dreams) could never afford. But thanks to generous people who left treasures to these institutions, we have the opportunity to view fabulous collections.

Let me tell you about a special patron of the Art Institute of Chicago, where my Gram took me when I was a boy. Visitors

An early view of the Chicago "castle" of Mrs. Potter Palmer, who gave most of her incredible art collection to the Art Institute of Chicago.

(Author's collection)

There's no better and enjoyable way to learn about antiques than visiting historic house/museums. Montpelier, in Orange, Virginia, is a learning feast.

(Photo courtesy of James Madison's Montpelier)

"[Late Residence of Ex-President Madison, Montpelier, Va.]"

Engraving, by unknown artist, c. 1836.

Courtesy of The Montpelier Foundation

can't help but admire the lady who bestowed so many outstanding artifacts to this grand museum. Her name was Mrs. Potter Palmer, and some of the treasures she so kindly donated included paintings by Edouard Manet and, as I mentioned earlier, Pierre Renoir. You might be familiar with her hus-

. . . .

Museum hopping is an excellent way to learn about antiques. You'll view dazzlers that most of us could never afford.

. . . .

band's legendary hotel and beloved Chicago landmark, the Palmer House. Other museums are also fortunate to have generous donors who make it possible for the public to enjoy one-of-a-kind collections.

So bring your glasses, wear walking shoes, forget that cursed cell phone, and be prepared to spend the whole day at your favorite museum. If walking through galleries makes you hungry, consider eating at a restaurant there. Most museums have excellent restaurants, so you really can spend an entire day.

A Visual Feast At Museums

In these halls of knowledge, displays give detailed information about each exhibited object. This gives you access to the accumulated knowledge of expert museum curators. When a description says the chair in front of you is mahogany, you have the opportunity to record the rich grain and auburn color in your memory for future reference. What a super way for learning. So read and look, read and look. I do this every time and often take notes, which you might want to do as well.

Museums will increase your knowledge, as this montage does about Victorian mementos at the Charleston Museum.

(Photo courtesy of Charleston Museum)

By visiting historic homes such as the Heyward-Washington House in Charleston, South Carolina, you will pick up knowledge about kitchen antiques.

(Photo courtesy of Charleston Museum)

Watch Those Alarms

You might be tempted to touch museum displays, but this is an absolute no-no. You must control your impulse, although this is harder than it sounds. Be forewarned that an object behind a rope or rail is also protected by sensitive alarms. So be careful about pointing too closely at what you are ogling. One time, as I was extolling the virtues of a 1700s French room to my students at the Cincinnati Art Museum, I set off an alarm twice! The second beeping gave the class, the guard, and me a big laugh, which seemed to humanize the very formal atmosphere. But I assure you, I kept my hands in my pockets for the rest of our tour.

Museum displays list detailed information to provide you with the accumulated knowledge of expert museum curators.

Museum Hopping On Trips

A friend once chided me that I was the only person she knew who returned from Florida paler than when he left. She was right. Rather than lying out on the beach, I visited museums all across the Sunshine State. And I would do it all again if given the chance. Always remember the knowledge that you acquire from those great places always stays with you, so do include some museum hopping while on your next vacation.

In museums, get as close as possible (without setting off alarms), so you can get really acquainted with first-class antiques.

(Photo courtesy of James Madison's Montpelier)

You just never know when something you absorb from a display may someday help you spot an unsung valuable.

Two Bibles For The Sensual Approach

In the late 1800s, Sears, Roebuck and Company, "the cheapest supply house on earth," and Montgomery Ward, both of Chicago, distributed their catalogues to residents in towns and farms all across the country. Both firms sold at very low prices, underselling most local businesses. Their selections were mammoth and offered anything a household could possibly need, from silver spoons to horse collars. The two retailers were the Wal-Marts and Targets of late nineteenth- and early twentieth-century America.

. . . .

Because the Sears and Wards catalogues record such a rich heritage of American products, they're a great resource for surveying antiques.

. . . .

Because the catalogues record such a rich heritage of American products, they're a great resource for surveying antiques. These fascinating texts, which I call "Bibles for the Sensual Approach to Learning," date back to the late 1800s. Incidentally, the original catalogues are no longer just a reference to antiques; they have justifiably become antiques themselves. But, you can buy inexpensive reproductions of their catalogues at bookstores.

The pages of the catalogues give us insights into the daily lives of our not-too-distant ancestors. One area I find particularly mesmerizing is the china section, which Sears called the "crockery department." Our forebears had a selection of dishes that could overwhelm even the most ardent modern-day china collector. Sears offered sets made by firms now considered the *Who's Who* of great British and French potters. Firms

Old magazines, like vintage catalogues, teach us so much about antiques.

(Author's collection)

such as Meakin and Wetherby, both of Hanley, England; Maddock of Great Britain; and Charles Field Haviland of France produced ceramics that are now highly esteemed antiques.

. . . .

The Sears and Ward catalogues are essentially hand-held museums. Use these time capsules to research delightful facts about all kinds of late-1800s and early 1900s antiques.

. . . .

Sears said that Haviland was "the largest manufacturer of china in the world and their name is sufficient guarantee of quality." A fifty-five-piece Haviland dinner service of six dinner plates, six teacups and saucers, a sugar bowl, a covered vegetable dish, and other pieces cost only $9. Today, you would be fortunate to purchase a single saucer for that price.

The Sears and Ward catalogues are essentially hand-held museums. You can find just about any antique in their pages. People are always writing to my newspaper column about their foot-operated sewing machines. Their interest leads me to believe that these early marvels of the machine age are cherished keepsakes for a great many Americans. If you have one, it's probably similar to those Sears offered in the 1897 edition of its catalogue. The "New Queen" model, listed at $22.50, was "guaranteed as the greatest value ever offered." Such a pitch must have created huge sales. Perhaps yours is similar to this ultra-high-tech model (for the 1890s), which even included an oak desk/cabinet.

If you're considering investing in an antique, these time capsules of American history can help you decide whether or not to buy. Use the catalogues to research delightful facts about all kinds of late-1800s and early 1900s antiques.

I seriously considered buying a small curio cabinet at a show but reluctantly decided to pass. When I looked in my

From an antiquer's point of view, *Gone With the Wind* is the best movie of all time.

(Photo courtesy of Skinner's Auction Company)

catalogue a few days later, I found a piece that was almost identical. It was described as a parlor cabinet made of birch (a very light-colored wood) with "imitation mahogany finish." When I discovered that the catalogue price was only $18, I was somewhat relieved that I hadn't bought the one I spotted at the show for $200.

Wouldn't it be wonderful if we could buy antiques at 1890s prices? Someday our descendants will probably wish they could buy their antiques at twenty-first-century prices. Get copies of these catalogues, and you'll have a grand time gaining practical knowledge about antiques.

Gone With The Wind: *An Antiques Tutor*

The Sensual Approach to Learning can appeal even to couch potatoes. Thanks to cable stations like Turner Classic Movies, which constantly runs old movies, television has become one of the best promoters of antiques. Whether the plots take place in previous centuries, the "mod" 1960s, or Retro 1970s, old flicks highlight furniture, china, and other antiques and decorating tastes from the past.

Gone With the Wind is a tremendous movie for many reasons; but from an antiques point of view, it tops the others by far. Its settings accurately depict how American homes went through a transition from the plainer furnishings of the pre-Civil War era to the supreme curlicue styles that were the last word in the 1860s. The next time you watch this 1939 cinematic masterpiece, be sure to note the more demure furniture and color schemes of Scarlet O'Hara's childhood home, Tara. Then contrast the plantation with her Peachtree Mansion built in Atlanta after the war. Her highly stylized house out-dazzled even the most ornate Victorian houses and vividly shows the dramatic change in decorating tastes taking place at this time. Pay special attention to the scene in which Captain Butler carries Miss Scarlet up the grand staircase. This highly charged scene showcases the grandeur of this home, which

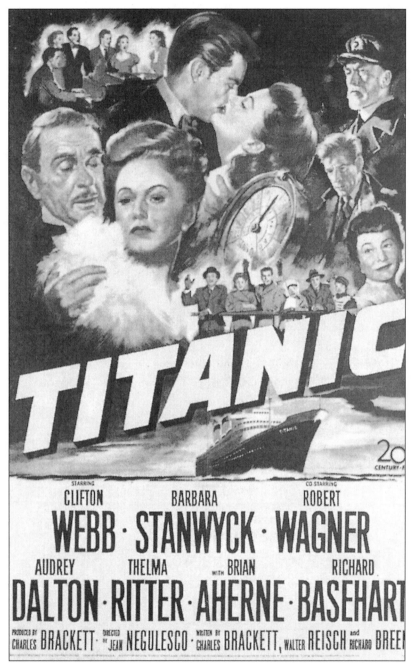

As you watch Barbara Stanwyck suffering ever so nobly in the 1953 movie *Titanic*, notice the lush furnishings of the 1912 luxury liner.

(Photo courtesy of Skinner's Auction Company)

was the antithesis of the more understated style at Tara. Characteristic Victorian elegance abounds in Peachtree Mansion in the form of stained glass windows, dark wood-work, velvet upholstery, ornate furniture, and cathedral-high ceilings.

. . . .

Old movies are such great instructors about antiques that you may end up rating them by the antiques they showcase in their interior scenes, rather than by their plots.

. . . .

Old movies are such great instructors about antiques that you may end up rating them by the antiques they showcase in their interior scenes, rather than by their plots. Many a time, I have loved a film when friends didn't because I was concentrating on the sets and ignoring the action. That's why I don't care for Westerns. They typically have little furniture and focus on the great outdoors. Why can't the producers throw a few more antiques into their scenes just to add some old-time ambiance for us viewers who also happen to be learning antiquers?

6

Which Goods Give the Best Value?

THE SENSUAL APPROACH TO WOODS

The Sensual Approach to Learning will help you evaluate antiques in detail. Using this method, you can determine a number of characteristics about a piece, including the type of wood it is made from. This is an essential skill because it can help you find pieces that are undervalued.

· ·

Being able to determine the type of wood a piece of furniture is made from is an essential skill because it can help you find pieces that are undervalued.

· ·

A humorous incident in my antiques class finally made me realize that antique furniture originally came from something growing in a forest. One day a student asked, "What kind of tree grows mahogany?" I stumbled for an answer because I had always thought of wood as the material used to make a chair or a table rather than as the substance that comes from a living tree. Then the answer to the student's question dawned on me. "A mahogany tree grows mahogany," I finally announced with much relief. His simple yet significant ques-

Antique furniture originated from trees like these captured in oils
by Austrian artist Carl Moll (1861-1945).

(Photo courtesy of Skinner's Auction Company of Boston)

tion illustrates the importance of recognizing woods. Being familiar with the main woods used to craft antique furniture will enable you to spot giveaways.

THREE CHEERS FOR VENEER

Before delving into woods, I'd like to correct the common perception that veneer means poor quality. On the contrary, just as chocolate icing makes a cake appear chocolate inside and out, veneer creates the same illusion with furniture. Anyone can nail boards together to make a stool, but the process of gluing a very thin layer of expensive wood over a more common one takes great skill. Veneer is a mark of craftsmanship, one that keeps prices in line by using rare woods sparingly.

With that in mind, let's move on to the "Big Six" of woods, which can be divided into three groups. These six woods, which are the most important and easiest to recognize, include two auburns (mahogany and cherry), one lone brunette (walnut), and three blonds (oak, maple, and pine). I also have a special treat for you—the secret of how the Christmas wood got its name.

The Auburns

MUSEUM-QUALITY MAHOGANY

Of the two auburn woods, mahogany is the one with the higher social status. It has a plain grain with a color similar to cordovan leather or rosé wine. Imported from the West Indies and Central America, it was customarily used for top-of-the-line furniture. By 1750, mahogany had become chic for high rollers in London, New York, Boston, and Charleston. This aristocrat of woods was mainly used for drawing-room or dining-room pieces in ritzy homes. Although most articles from that era are now museum caliber, you'll soon have a strategy to buy antiques crafted in this blue-blood wood.

NON-MUSEUM MAHOGANY

Twentieth-century mahogany copies of eighteenth-century models enchantingly combine pedigreed style with collector-friendly prices. The semi-antiques/collectibles often follow designs of Thomas Chippendale (1718-1779), who in his time was as famous a designer as Ralph Lauren is today. Quality machine-made chairs from the 1930s and 1940s copied the Englishman's trademarks right down to his famous hand carved ball-and-claw feet mentioned in Chapter 5.

This circa 1830 chest over drawers was grained to look like mahogany.

(Photo courtesy of Skinner's Auction Company)

Remember how your posterior revealed mahogany's density? Fortunately, this trait can be a benefit to the cabinetmaker (the proper term for a furniture maker). Mahogany's strength made it possible for craftsmen to carve ball-and-claw feet and other designs with great detail.

Pursue semi-antique/collectible examples from the last century duplicating 1700s designs if you want to give your home a highbrow, landed-gentry atmosphere without landed-gentry prices.

· ·

Pursue semi-antique/collectibles duplicating 1700s designs if you want to give your home a highbrow, landed-gentry atmosphere without landed-gentry prices.

· ·

CHERRY

Cherry, the second auburn, is probably the most beloved wood. It grew almost everywhere in the United States and was popular for many rural pieces. You'll notice that cherry resembles mahogany but with a slightly paler color—more like a blush wine. Cherry provided the strength country folks needed for durable furnishings. These days, it's easy to forget cherry's humble origin because it gives mahogany a run for big antiques bucks.

This early 1800s sugar chest from the Mary Todd Lincoln House in Lexington, Kentucky, shows cherry at its best.

(Photo courtesy of Mary Todd Lincoln House)

More cherry pieces from the Mary Todd Lincoln House.

(Photo courtesy of Mary Todd Lincoln House)

Cherry offers another bonus. Sometimes, along with its pinkish grain, you can detect a champagne-colored vein resembling a streak of lightning. This vivid mix of rose and off-white adds pizzazz to rural pieces, which tended to be plainer looking compared to their urban counterparts.

THE AUBURN NEAR TWINS

Because mahogany and cherry were considered almost twins, thrifty cabinetmakers used both on early 1800s furniture. Often, they cleverly incorporated cherry on the sides of chests and saved the costlier mahogany veneers for the fronts. Thus, the piece looked as if it were made entirely of mahogany, helping cherry become known as "the poor man's mahogany." Ironically, it should now be called "the affluent collector's wood" because cherry pieces can cost as much as mahogany versions, but shortly you'll learn how to acquire cherry furniture without going broke.

The Lone Brunette

WALNUT

Walnut, the only brunette of the "Big Six," is universally loved and grows around the world. Like chocolate fudge, walnut can be found in a full range of shades from light to dark. Walnut's porous grain makes it very durable. Before 1720, walnut was a favorite choice for European and American furniture. In the 1800s, American country pieces such as beds and tables were frequently made from walnut.

Why has walnut been so popular? Think of it as the navy-blue blazer of woods. Although blue blazers aren't on the cutting edge of fashion, they're practical and always in style. Like that wardrobe classic, walnut works well in virtually any setting or century. Another bonus is that walnut is far more affordable than cherry and mahogany.

The Blonds

OAK

The most famous blond is oak, which grows in Britain and the United States. English oak tends to be darker than its American counterpart because of climatic differences. Its durability made it a natural choice for the construction of houses and ships, as well as furniture. In fact, before the 1700s,

Here's a look at early 1900s oak crafted by Gustav Stickley, whose style is often called "Craftsman" or "Mission."

(Photo courtesy of Skinner's Auction Company)

This circa 1910 table is a great example of "golden oak."

(Photo courtesy of Middletown Journal)

oak and walnut were the chief woods for British and European furniture. Of all of the woods, oak is the easiest to recognize. Rub your fingers along a piece to feel its lively grain. Like most blonds, oak comes in various shades from Chablis to stout beer.

GOLDEN OAK

"Golden oak" refers to American furniture made around 1900. Those round dining tables with carved, hairy animal claw feet that you have probably seen were frequently made from this wood. The aging oak finish in time takes on a lovely, deep amber, giving birth to its charming name.

My 1897 catalogue advertised a golden oak hallstand complete with built-in bench, hooks, and mirrored section for $7.50. Those certainly were the "good old days" because in a shop today you would probably have to pay from a hundred to two hundred times its 1897 price!

MAPLE

Maple trees are widespread throughout the world, with the Vermont varieties celebrated for their sweet syrup. Maple wood ranges in color from off-white to a light-golden tone. At first, you may find it difficult to spot its fine grain, but in no time at all you'll be able to distinguish its slight veining. Give

The legs of this 1810 work table are mahogany, while the drawer front is bird's-eye maple.

(Photo courtesy of Skinner's Auction Company)

a piece of maple a good rap with your knuckles and you'll feel its strength and solidity. That's the reason this blond was mainly used for rural pieces and rarely was carved.

. . . .

Maple was crafted into country furniture from the American Revolution to about 1900. It remains an excellent choice for chair legs and cutting boards because of its great durability.

. . . .

In the United States, maple was crafted into country furniture from the American Revolution to about 1900. You've probably seen maple ladderback chairs from the 1800s that tout this wood's rich color and grain. Maple remains an excellent choice for chair legs and cutting boards because of its great durability.

ANOTHER PLUG FOR VENEER

Bird's-eye maple veneer got its name from the swirling designs created by the knots in the wood. Cabinetmakers were able to dress up plain-looking walnut and cherry chests of drawers by gluing thin strips of this veneer to their drawer fronts. This process was also much easier than carving decorations, which took great skill and much sweat before machine production.

MAPLE MEANS CHAMPAGNE

These days, maple is very trendy, which greatly increases its price. A 1700s table can sell at auction for double what a comparable cherry or mahogany one would fetch. Even twentieth-century maple pieces cost more than their cherry or mahogany counterparts. (Now you grasp why the $295 dinette set in Chapter 1 was such a steal.) Don't let high prices deter you, though. After learning a few tricks later on, you'll be able to afford maple pieces.

THE CHRISTMAS WOOD

Every December, many of us decorate this blond, and in the true spirit of Christmas, it bears many gifts. Yes, I'm referring to pine, a tree common to Europe and North America. Become familiar with this wood by surveying its very pale and vibrant graining. Once considered low end—the spaghetti of timber—pine is now in vogue. In the past, pine was veneered, painted, or hidden on the back and inside of furniture. George Washington even had his pine walls in Mount Vernon grain-painted to make his foyer appear paneled in more upscale mahogany. Now, pine, like spaghetti, has gained prestige. Spaghetti is no longer relegated to a blue-plate special but is revered as "pasta," and is served in a variety of ways at the finest restaurants. Similarly, pine is now considered trendy, but it remains the Christmas wood because it gives the most gifts.

GIFT #1: AFFORDABILITY

The pine tree's festive evergreen boughs and fragrant aroma not only lifts our spirits but offers another morale-boosting present. While maple, cherry, and mahogany antiques are high-ticket items, pine gives a lot more for your antiques dollars. A 1900 pine cupboard costs much less than similar versions in other timbers. Pine's affordability is one reason why it has justly come into its own.

LOOMISM
Pine is the Christmas wood because it gives the gift of beauty, practicality, and comfort at an affordable price.

GIFT #2: NEUTRAL COLOR

Pine's neutral color goes well with other woods. The Christmas timber mixes happily in your home with furniture crafted from various woods. Maple and oak blend well with other woods, too, but for more money.

Gift #3: Dust Camouflage

My Gram pointed out another perk of pine's light coloring: It doesn't show dust like darker woods. Other blonds like oak offer the same advantage but are higher end.

. . . .

Pine is affordable, comfortable, neutral in color, and hides dust better than darker woods.

. . . .

Gift #4: Comfort

In the Sensual Approach to Learning, I suggested that you use your posterior to compare a mahogany seat with a pine seat. That will give you first-hand appreciation for one of pine's most prized traits—comfort. After you've tried this experiment, it should be obvious why this softwood is a favorite for chair seats.

Staining and Varnishing

A few words about stain and varnish will enhance your knowledge about furniture. Stain is a weak, paint-like solution applied to wood to duplicate the color of another wood. Cabinetmakers commonly used stain to try to make a piece of furniture look as if it were made entirely from a single type of wood.

Rarely did this process completely succeed, however. Mahogany stain usually took on an iodine-red hue. Maple, all the rage during the Early American craze of the 1950s (like the furnishings in the Ricardo's Connecticut house in *I Love Lucy*) tended to develop an orange tone. Cherry became garish pink, while oak became far too dark. Only walnut, the blue-blazer wood, usually escaped staining. Because the dyes found in stains can camouflage or "hide" the wood, it is tricky to recognize its graining underneath, but soon I'll give you tips for overcoming this challenge.

While staining changed the color of the wood, it didn't preserve it. Another material, varnish, was needed to provide protection. This solution of resins of alcohol or linseed oil was applied on stained or unstained surfaces to create a transparent but impenetrable coat much the same way a piece of glass protects a framed print.

THE SENSUAL APPROACH TO LEARNING WOODS
Touring Lumberyards

To master the various types of raw (unstained) timbers, visit lumberyards. And while your fingers are exploring the grains and textures, enjoy the intoxicating aroma of the lumber. The smell of cut wood is as pleasant as freshly mowed grass and linen dried in the sun. Then store those intense sensory impressions in the scrapbook of your mind for future reference. You'll need to call on those mental notes to help identify the woods you'll encounter while searching for antiques.

Marquetry is an inlay or veneer of rare woods depicting designs like these on this 1800 Italian chest of drawers.

(Photo courtesy of Skinner's Auction Company)

Visiting Stores, Shows, and Museums

Go antiquing to find walnut, cherry, oak, maple, pine, and mahogany pieces. Stay alert and pay careful attention to the accompanying descriptions. These are learning opportunities not to be missed. Closely examine and caress various wooden articles. Learn their color, grain, and feel. You will be surprised at the uniqueness of the texture of each type of wood.

Exploring Museums

While it's necessary for museums to keep their masterpieces out of reach, it's frustrating for those who want to practice the Sensual Approach. But even though treasures can't be touched, a museum's superb displays and descriptions provide unparalleled opportunities for learning. Read—look at the object—scan the description again—take a final look—and, as I warned you earlier, be sure to avoid the alarms! In just a few hours at a museum, you can absorb a great deal that will be useful for antiquing later.

. . . .

Closely examine and caress various wooden articles. Learn their color, grain, and feel. You will be surprised at the uniqueness of the texture of each type of wood.

. . . .

Remember, the value of antique furniture depends in large part on the wood used and the period in which they were made. Keep this handy reference with you when you visit malls, shows, shops, and dime stores.

∾

WOODS AND BUCKS:
A COMPARISON OF AMERICAN FURNITURE PRICES
BY TYPE OF WOOD

PRE-1700S (PRE-EIGHTEENTH CENTURY)

Walnut	$$$$
Oak	$$$$
Pine	$$

1700S (EIGHTEENTH CENTURY)

Mahogany	$$$$
Maple	$$$$
Walnut	$$$
Oak	$$
Pine	$

1800S (NINETEENTH CENTURY)

Mahogany	$$$$
Maple	$$$$
Walnut	$$$
Oak	$$
Pine	$

1900S (TWENTIETH CENTURY)

Oak	$$$$
Maple	$$$$
Mahogany	$$$
Walnut	$$$
Pine	$

PART IV

THE SPORT OF BARGAINING

7

Becoming an Antiques Jock

PRICE NEGOTIATION IS THE SPORT FOR GETTING AFFORDABLE ANTIQUES

Before you learn anything else about antiques, you must master the game of price negotiation. No matter where you shop, this skill is crucial to your success as a bargain antiquer. Keep in mind that everyone from seller to collector expects to negotiate prices. Knowing that most of us are expected and are quite eager to bargain should make you feel more comfortable and give you the incentive to become a pro at this sport.

. . . .

You must master the sport of price negotiation.
This skill is crucial to your success as a bargain antiquer.
Knowing that most of us are expected to bargain
should make you feel more comfortable and
help you become a pro.

. . . .

By following my antiquer-and-seller-friendly strategies, you'll save bundles. Best of all, you'll be able to do so stress-free. Soon you'll know how to apply Loomisms to get terrific buys whether you're antiquing at shows, malls, shops, flea markets, garage sales, or thrift stores.

BRAVO, ANTIQUES DEALERS

The best dealers and auctioneers are our friends. They work hard to make their merchandise look so beguiling.

(Photo courtesy of Garth's Auctions, Inc.)

Before you venture into the bargaining world, we need to give a round of applause to antiques dealers. Successful dealers work hard and deserve to make a profit. Their days are spent finding merchandise, preparing it for display, paying insurance and rent, and working with demanding people like us. By appreciating their work, and regarding them as friends, you'll be able to make negotiation an even more pleasant experience.

THREE INGREDIENTS FOR
SUCCESSFUL NEGOTIATION
Honey/Gentility

Your victory (getting great prices without sacrificing quality) depends on your demeanor during the transaction. My Aunt Panny often said, "You catch more flies with honey than vinegar." She taught me by example that the finest deals are made by being genteel. Kind expressions can roll back prices faster than harsh ones ever could. Carefully choosing your words and tone is essential to creating the proper bargaining environment. For example, the term "negotiating" has a much more positive connotation than "haggling." Delete other negative words from your bargaining vocabulary to promote harmony and get the lowest prices.

. . . .

My Aunt Panny taught me that kind words can roll back prices faster than harsh ones ever could.

. . . .

My successful antiquing through the years has proved Aunt Panny right about so many things, and especially about this issue. At the risk of sounding like a relic from the Kennedy era, please use your best manners while wheeling and dealing. I have heard scores of sellers say that they didn't come down in price because they resented how rudely a person treated them. Customers would be far better off if they realized that dealers are much more agreeable to lowering prices when they are treated with courtesy.

Humor

A light touch can put everyone in a cordial mood during a bargaining session. A laugh or a chuckle does more to relieve tension than a pitcher of martinis. Humor helps fill the awkward silent seconds while you await the outcome of a request such as, "Make me an offer I can't refuse."

A few years ago while antiquing in a village in southern France, I said that line in my best French. The dealer laughingly told me that she really enjoyed my style of bargaining and that she especially appreciated that I did so in her native tongue. Nonetheless, things became serious again, and she answered with the easily understood reply, "Non." Then my American-born friend, Becky, came to my aid by saying in superb French, "But he made you laugh. That should be worth something." That won the dealer over, and with a beaming smile, she agreed to reduce the price by fifty francs (about $9). Humor, like pets and antiques, crosses language and cultural barriers and can work wonders.

LOOMISM
Price negotiation is a sport, not a war. This attitude will help you get the best possible prices for whatever catches your antiques fancy.

Wardrobe

Gram taught me that clothes make the person. I would like to elaborate on that statement and say that clothes also make the antiquer. This doesn't mean you have to shop for your wardrobe at Brooks Brothers or Saks Fifth Avenue. However, when antiquing, wear apparel that makes you appear reasonably prosperous. Why? A dealer will be more willing to negotiate if you look as though you can afford the antique that has caught your interest.

THE ANTIQUES JOCK PLAYING THE SPORT OF NEGOTIATION
Making a Good First Impression

Always be ready with a friendly greeting for a dealer, antiques mall employee, or seller at an informal mart. Your cordiality will get you off to a good start, which in turn will establish a favorable atmosphere for all concerned when the conversation turns toward prices.

Shunning Out-of-the-Ballpark Prices

When an antique strikes your fancy, but the price is ridiculously high, don't waste time trying to get a better price. You'll have little success if the figure is inflated from the start. Be patient, look elsewhere, and you'll be amazed at how quickly something else will grab your attention.

Opening with the Pause Technique

My favorite first step is the pause technique. Try a variation of the following opener: "I really like this chair. Can you tell me any more about it to whet my appetite?" The question sends the message that you're interested. Follow with a long, silent pause. Your lull will give the dealer the chance to give a sales pitch and utter the words, "I can do better." You'll be astonished how often this occurs. If the dealer gives you a good price, accept it. But if you think it's still too high, give a counteroffer (explained below).

If the Pause Technique Strikes Out

If the seller doesn't offer a better price, you have to work a little more energetically. Try asking one of the following questions:

1. "I don't mean to insult you, but do you negotiate?"
2. "Is there any room for negotiation on your price?"
3. "Can you make me an offer I can't refuse?"

LOOMISM

The three negotiation lines combined with honey/gentility, humor, and proper wardrobe are exceptionally effective at lowering prices.

Respecting Firm Prices

One time after I asked question #2, a dealer responded, "What a lovely way to ask, but no." Her charming and diplomatic answer brings up an important point—sometimes the prices quoted are firm. Non-negotiable prices are unusual because sellers routinely mark merchandise with prices higher than they expect to get. Dealers generally adopt this policy because they know that most antiquers expect to negotiate, but some dealers only offer fixed prices. Right from the begin-

. . . .

If a dealer offers a good price, accept it.
But if you think it's still too high,
give a counteroffer.

. . . .

ning, they display their goods with the lowest price they'll accept. When a dealer says a price is firm, that means don't waste time or emotions trying to get a further reduction. It's up to you to accept or reject that figure as is. If this happens, use the "Stall Technique" below to give you time to decide whether to purchase at the stated price.

Making Counteroffers

What should you do when your charm, humor, wardrobe, and good lines have reduced the price, yet you still yearn for a bigger discount? Offer 20 to 25 percent less than the last figure. Do it, of course, with smiles and kindness. Dealers are usually insulted by an offer of 50 percent or less of the price, so avoid that approach. You'll rarely get that much of a discount and will probably just create hostility. A later chapter reveals how, under certain circumstances, you can safely ask (and probably get) a markdown of 50 percent or more.

THREE SHREWD BUYING TACTICS
Try "Two-for Deals"

If you want two items from one dealer, ask, "What price can you offer if I buy these two antiques from you?" A slight variation is to get an antiquing buddy (who is interested in purchasing an item from the same merchant) involved in this "two-for" tactic. Purchasing more than one antique at a time from the same seller can reduce prices. After all, other stores commonly have sales offering one item at the regular price and the second for half. So why not ask for the same deal at an antiques shop?

Buy Small First

A renowned dealer taught me this procedure when I was a twenty-something collector. This brainchild may just net you some uptown antiques at bargain basement prices. How? First, buy an inexpensive item for the asking figure. That small purchase not only makes you a customer but a dear, full-paying client in the seller's heart. This status practically guarantees a better price on future, more expensive purchases. You'll be dumbfounded at how this strategy rarely fails once the negotiation game begins.

. . . .

Paying full price for an inexpensive item practically guarantees a better price on a future, more expensive purchase.

. . . .

Use the Stall Technique

If you're unsure whether a final price is satisfactory, ask the seller or mall employee to hold the item for a day or two. It's more difficult to do this at a one-day show, flea market, or garage sale, but at most other venues it's a commonly accepted practice. This savvy strategy gives you time to determine if the price is fair. Just follow the comparison shopping guidelines detailed in Chapter 9.

Mistakes to Avoid

Before you test your negotiation skills, read and heed the following warnings. By knowing what not to do wherever you shop, you'll look like a first-stringer at this sport. This list of no-nos pertains mainly to situations in which you are speaking face-to-face with the seller.

THE $10/$5 RULE

When an item is marked $10 or less at shows or shops, don't ask for a discount. Even though you're not ashamed of being tight-fisted, you don't have to advertise this fact to the whole world. Besides, you might soon discover a more expensive and more enticing antique from the same dealer. As I mentioned earlier, paying full price for a tidbit makes a favorable impression and can increase the influence you have in your next transaction. At garage sales, flea markets, etc., refrain from asking for a reduction on items marked $5 or less.

Always be the antiques jock. That means to avoid negotiating if the price is under $10.

(Author's collection)

No Poor Mouthing

Poor mouthing, or complaining about your lack of funds, isn't a good way to get better prices. If you become cash poor, which happens to most of us from time to time, don't whine about it in public. Airing your dirty laundry won't get you sympathy. It's better to say, "I had hoped to stay within my budget." Sellers show little, if any, interest in negotiating with someone who appears to lack the resources to make a deal.

Never Question Expertise

If an item is described as "early Goodwill," but you think it is "late Salvation Army," don't challenge the dealer's knowledge. This only results in hurt feelings. It's unlikely you'll be able to get a favorable deal after insulting the seller. It is wiser to look elsewhere if you doubt the dealer's expertise.

Never Say, "I'll Give You..."

Most sellers consider the phrase, "I'll give you XXX dollars" condescending. They feel such a comment is unacceptable at stores owned by Mr. Bloomingdale and Mr. Walton, so why would it be appropriate to say to a dealer? This remark closes the door to price negotiation faster than popcorn bowls get emptied on Super Bowl Sunday.

Don't Knock the Merchandise

Years ago, before appraising totally took over my work, I used to conduct estate sales. A potential buyer once held up an item and sighed, "I would love to buy this bowl, Mr. Loomis, but it has a crack." (It didn't. If it had been broken, it would have been priced accordingly.) I replied, "In that case, I don't think I could sleep tonight if I sold it to you." From the seller's perspective, I have learned that knocking the merchandise is not a good way for a buyer to get lower prices. In fact, in this

LOOMISM

Buyers respond to charm and humor from the seller, too. Keep that in mind, so you don't get snowed and pay too much.

instance, because of my tactful answer, the customer bought the bowl and paid more than what he had intended. This

. . . .

I have learned from the seller's perspective that
knocking the merchandise is not a good way
for a seller to try to get a lower price.

. . . .

account illustrates how important charm and humor are to both sides of the negotiating table. A happy ending for both buyer and seller sets the stage for future successful price negotiations.

THE MONEY SPORT AT ANTIQUE MALLS

Because the dealers/owners aren't usually present at antique malls, price negotiation is rarely done on a shopper-to-dealer basis. However, you can still expect victorious antiquing because mall employees act like real estate agents who work between the owners and buyers, rendering the whole process less emotional. When you enter an antiques mall, check its policy on discounts. You can usually get a 10 percent discount on items over $10 or $20, but you usually have to ask for it. If a bigger reduction is your goal, the following Loomism will get you many home runs in the game of negotiation.

LOOMISM

At antiques malls, apply the same positive tactics for price negotiation that you use when bartering with a dealer face to face. Your charming approach towards mall employees will help you get friendlier prices.

I have learned this insider's secret from pals who own malls: because many proprietors charge dealers a percentage of their gross sales, mall personnel are naturally most obliging to let the antiques jock get into action. If you want more than 10 percent off a big-ticket item, ask the cashier if this is possible, using, of course, a variation of my three best lines.

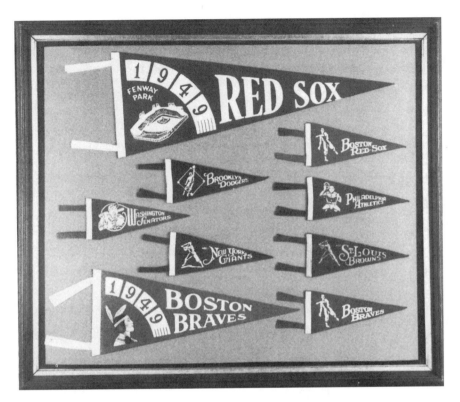

Don't be afraid to offer a lower price, using one of the previous suggestions, if you think your bid is fair.

A Travel Tip

While we're discussing malls and shops, I'd like to suggest a way to liven up long, tedious road trips and increase opportunities for antiquing at the same time. Take a break from driving by exploring the antiques malls appearing along so many expressways these days, or perhaps visit shops that are just a short distance from the exits.

At one of those super malls, I met a honeymooning older couple who were on a nonstop "antique-a-thon." They told me they had started in Kansas and were on their way to Pennsylvania, hitting practically every expressway mall between their house and their son's. Their antiquing appears to have been quite productive; their car was bursting with

These 1949 Red Sox baseball pennants are semi-antique/collectibles. Antiquing is indeed a sport.

(Photo courtesy of Skinner's Auction Company)

everything from chairs to enticing looking bundles. So when you're hungry, need gas, or just need to stretch your legs, scout for an antiques mall or nearby shops for a relaxing diversion.

. . . .

Don't buy an item if the bargaining process becomes unpleasant. You only want positive emotions associated with your antiques.

. . . .

Feng Shui and Bargaining

No matter where you are, don't buy an item if the bargaining process becomes unpleasant. Remember the principle of Feng Shui. If, every time you look at your antique, it recalls the tension caused by a rough negotiation session, then its purpose is defeated. If things get loathsome during bartering, it's best not to buy. You want only good vibes to be associated with your antiques so they'll embellish your home with positive energy.

Here's hoping the new owner of this 1915 oak table had fun acquiring it.

(Photo courtesy of Skinner's Auction Company)

A Dignified Exit

No matter at what locale the bargaining takes place, keep your cool throughout the entire process. If the price of an item remains unmoved after bargaining, it is better not to buy it. If the item remains too champagne (even after my best efforts at getting a good price), I save face with the following exit line: "I'm not in the same league as that antique, but I certainly hope it goes to a good home." If a similar situation happens to you, use your own variation of this line to get off the antiques hook with honor.

Don't Jump the Gun

Another point to remember. We all feel at times that a certain antique is the only one like it in the universe. This is usually—and thankfully—a mistake. That beauty you crave is more common than you think. Although antiques are less plentiful than their brand-new counterparts, they have been around a long time and are more abundant than you can imagine. So have faith! Sooner or later you will find the antique of your dreams, perhaps at a far better price.

LOOMISM

Remember, there are many antiques in the sea of life!

PART V

BARGAINS 'R US

8

"Woolworth's" for Budget Antiquers in Training

GARAGE SALES, FLEA MARKETS AND THRIFT STORES: BONANZAS FOR NOVICES

You're now ready to practice the negotiating principles you've been learning. In a short time, you'll be able to make bigger purchases, but before diving into the deep end of the antiquing pool, you should test the waters by dipping your

Outdoor antiques markets/flea markets offer great antiquing possibilities.

(Photo courtesy of Queen City Shows)

toes into the shallow end. This means shopping in less-than-posh markets—garage sales, flea markets, and thrift stores. These are the best places for budget antiquers to practice. Let's call these cut-rate outlets "Woolworth's" in honor of the famous dime-store chain started in 1879 that was synonymous for value.

ANTIQUES CEILINGS

Before we discuss these affordable marketplaces, I'd like to introduce my Antiques Ceilings—simplified price guides that will allow you to shop with complete peace of mind. I created these references to give you an extra level of protection. I have included an Antiques Ceiling for every category of antiques highlighted in this primer. Each entry lists the maximum amount you should pay for various items.

. . . .

Before diving into the deep end of the antiquing pool, you should test the waters by dipping your toes into the shallow end. This means shopping in less-than-posh markets— garage sales, flea markets, and thrift stores. These are the best places for budget antiquers to practice.

. . . .

YOUR ANTIQUES CEILINGS FOR "WOOLWORTH'S"

Consider any antique a major purchase if it costs more than $35. Limit your purchases to this amount for the time being when shopping at "Woolworth's." This should greatly reduce any trepidation you might have about being sold the Brooklyn Bridge or being taken for an antiques ride.

A RELIABLE PRICE GUIDE

Once you've developed some antiques expertise, you'll be ready to find deals. When you reach that point, you'll need one more tool—*Warman's Antiques and Collectibles Price Guide*. I firmly believe every collector needs a copy of this excellent reference book. Without doubt, during your excursions you'll find unfamiliar antiques flirting with you. No need to fear being snookered because *Warman's* will be your guardian angel. Let's suppose, for instance, that a beautiful soup tureen marked "Limoges" beckons to you. Just flip to the Limoges section of *Warman's* to get an estimate of what you should pay for French china from the late 1800s. With the help of *Secrets to Affordable Antiques* and *Warman's*, you'll become a stellar antiquer.

SENSUAL TESTING FOR SAFE ANTIQUING

In Chapter 5, I presented the Sensual Approach to Learning, which is a hands-on method of study. As you recall, it's based on reading the descriptions of fine antiques in upscale establishments and museums and internalizing that information through the senses. It includes touching, caressing, ogling, and

The filled parking lot at this outdoor show lot proves the popularity of outdoor shows.

(Photo courtesy of Queen City Shows)

even sitting on various antiques to experience them firsthand and cement their characteristics in your memory.

Sensual Testing for Safe Antiquing, a continuation of the Sensual Approach to Learning, provides you with an additional safety net. This process should eliminate any apprehension you may feel about shopping at "Woolworth's." In fact, you'll find no better place to carry out negotiation tactics. But before you begin practicing, carefully review all the steps of Sensual Testing for Safe Antiquing.

When you stumble on a beauty at one of these outlets, chances are good that you're on your own when it comes to determining authenticity. Rarely will you find any information about the merchandise, and any data that is available could be suspect. Although at first this might seem to be a drawback, by using your senses you may be able to find some spectacular deals overlooked by others.

. . . .

By relying on your senses at "Woolworth's," you may be able to find spectacular deals overlooked by others.

. . . .

Shop anywhere you fancy—flea markets, estate sales, or garage sales. It doesn't matter as long as you do your antiques sleuthing. There's no need for self-doubt even though you haven't read mountains of reference books. The studying you've done in museums and first-rate retail stores, plus what you are learning here, will help prepare you for this challenge.

SENSUAL TESTING IN ACTION
Your Eyes

Let's say you spot a footstool with what you think are the highly touted cabriole legs that so captivated you in shops and museums. Closing your eyes, and peering into your mental file, you find classic examples you have studied. If those versions match the on-site example, bravo! You have verified that they are indeed cabriole legs. Now use your newly developed negotiating skills to complete the transaction.

. . . .

To identify antiques, close your eyes and peer into your mental file to find classic examples you have studied.

. . . .

Your Fingers

Perhaps a table captivates you. Its carved ball-and-claw feet pique your interest and are similar to those you have seen during your learning expeditions. You're doing well. As an antiques investigator, give one of the feet a massage. This will help you determine whether it is made from one solid piece of wood or several glued together. Close your eyes to focus your concentration as you rub your fingers over the carving, which depicts a bird's claw holding a large pearl. If the carving feels detailed and fully dimensional, it is made from a single block of wood. This indicates that you've discovered a top-notch, handmade table. Its fine pedigree and your singing heart motivate you to negotiate for a sweeter price.

If your examination has left you somewhat dubious about the table's identity, look elsewhere. Maybe you'll find some intriguing china around the corner. If you find a piece especially appealing because you think it might be hand painted, do the touch test. If the decoration feels nubby from hand-dabbed paint, grab it. On the other hand, if you detect little or no stubbiness, it's probably more recent, so let it pass.

Your Derriere Again

I have a thing for unmatched antique chairs because they're so downright affordable (more about this in Chapter 15). A stylish chair can easily seduce me, especially if it has extraordinary cabriole legs and a terrific price. That combination usu-ally hooks me, and then I'm ready to engage in serious price negotiation. At that stage I usually hear my grandmother ask-ing, "Frankie, is it comfortable?" or my antiquing chum, Pete, very bluntly directing me to "Sit on it." Either comment reminds me to practice what I preach to prevent me from making an antiques boo-boo. So remember to give any poten-tial chair purchase the rump test. The chair may be gorgeous and a great buy, but what good is that if it isn't comfortable?

Always Read Your "Bible"

The reproductions of old catalogues I mentioned earlier are veritable warehouses of facts about the antiques sold at "Woolworth's." These references can even help you research a potential find before you turn over any of your hard-earned money. At these "bargain basements," it's unlikely that a seller will hold an item for you. But do try (using the honey approach) because you just might be surprised. This will give you time to rush home and review your catalogues for more information. You just might find critical data to help you make a wise decision.

Not too long ago at a flea market, your antiques coach bought a table just like the one at top left for $10, which was $3.50 less than its 1946 price!

(Author's collection)

If an item passed your Sensual Test, but the seller refuses to hold it for you, what's there to lose but $35 (or less) as out-lined in the Antiques Ceiling for "Woolworth's." Perhaps your pride will be bruised if you make a mistake, but we've all goofed. That's just part of the sport. Besides, what you learn from the experience will help you be more successful in the

future. This is a drawback of shopping in informal outlets, but the benefits far outnumber risks, provided you follow the guidelines.

. . . .

If a seller will place an item on hold for you, you'll have time to rush home and review catalogues for more information.

. . . .

If you purchased the item, you'll naturally want to learn more about it. This may require more than merely checking manuals in the library. Most reference and coffee-table books only illustrate pristine museum-quality antiques, which very few of us can afford. So it can be rather frustrating trying to unearth any more data about your prize, but I have a fun way of doing this research.

Tables are among the most charming and useful items found at informal markets. *(Author's collection)*

Recently I bought a little maple table with one drawer (and cabriole legs!) which, when brand new, was a vanity or dressing table. Its original attached mirror had been lost, thereby reducing its price to $100. What a boon that flaw proved; not only did I get a deal, but a perfect table for my office as well.

. . . .

Most of your purchases from "Woolworth's" will date from the 1890s through the 1970s, the heyday for Sears and Wards catalogues.

. . . .

Although this find will never be highlighted in any upscale book, that's just fine. Why? Because it already appeared in a Sears catalogue over a hundred years ago! Here's another example of how vintage catalogues come to the rescue of antiquers everywhere. Now you can fully appreciate why I call them "bibles." In this case, I found a comparable model in my 1897 issue. How fascinating to discover that in those days it was called a "toilet table," which doesn't mean what you may be thinking. The English word "toilet" came from the French term "toilette," meaning dressing table or vanity.

My research further revealed that back then, Sears didn't call cabriole legs by their loftier sounding French name. The Chicago retailer probably thought the word "cabriole" sounded too foreign, making it too intimidating for most Americans to pronounce. Sales experts decided that if customers couldn't pronounce it, they wouldn't buy it, so the word "cabriole" was replaced by the phrase "French bent legs." In the twenty-first century, the $100 price tag doesn't seem too high when compared to its nineteenth-century "special price of $10."

Most of your purchases from "Woolworth's" will date from the 1890s through the 1970s, the heyday for these catalogues. How appropriate it seems to use Sears and Wards catalogues to research "Woolworth's" antiques. In the early 1900s, the three businesses engaged in a rivalry similar to the current one among Wal-Mart, Target, and other large chain stores.

Stardom for Antiques

My students and radio listeners have enthusiastically told me they often recognize antiques similar to ones they've seen in movies or television shows. As I admitted earlier, I'm not a big fan of Westerns, but I am warming towards this genre for a good reason—they have immortalized a special china pattern.

All of us have undoubtedly watched countless flicks depicting the Old West. Hollywood leads us to believe that most indoors meals were served on blue-and-white Willow pattern china. Even television has joined in the act. Have you ever noticed Angela Lansbury's dishes on *Murder, She Wrote?* If you find china resembling her set decorated with a willow tree, lovebirds, and two pagodas, pat yourself on the back while snatching them up.

Famous Noritake china from Japan turns up regularly at "Woolworth's."
(Photo courtesy of Middletown Journal)

Your Instincts

Imagine you encounter another charming piece of china. Its decoration looks old, has texture, and has passed the first part of your Sensual Testing evaluation with flying colors. As you continue your examination, you turn it over to scrutinize its mark, but you find it impossible to read because it's so blurry and sloppy. Your experience at shops and museums has proven that most first-class marks, even if hazy, can usually be read, which is impossible with this example.

. . . .

Most first-class marks, even if hazy, can usually be read. Impossible-to-read marks send up a red flag that says, "Fake." When this happens, pass on the item in question. Remember, there are many more antiques in the sea of life!

. . . .

Your reaction sends up a red flag. You recall that you've seen similar impossible-to-read marks on reproductions in department stores. Your gut feeling yells, "Fake" because it resembles those copies, so you reject the set. What a wise decision! Remember that there are many antiques in the sea of life. However, if your instincts strongly suggest that the set is genuine, then buy it.

A Brainy Discussion

Another safety net forces you to evaluate an item objectively. Ask yourself, "Do I really need or want this, or am I just buying it to have the satisfaction of getting something?" Notice that I don't raise the issue of where it is going in your house. You'll learn how to solve that problem when you learn how to de-clutter your home in Chapter 12. There you'll discover painless ways to provide space for new finds while earning money to help pay for them.

The Final Umpire: Your Heart

Whether the antique is priceless or practically being given away, your heart must make the final decision. As Monsieur Renoir advised, only buy what gives you joy. If you purchase what makes your heart sing, you'll acquire all the high-spirited perks antiques offer.

"Cat-Tail" ceramic kitchenware from the 1940s is fun to find at garage sales.

(Author's collection)

That's all the guidance you need for safe antiquing at "Woolworth's." Because these outlets typically have low overhead and lack expertise in antiques, they sometimes offer miraculous prices for bargain hunters. So let's take a look at the various "Woolworth's" available to antiquers.

GARAGE SALES: BOUNTY IN YOUR NEIGHBORHOOD

Garage sales are widespread and, of course, are usually found in garages, and on driveways and lawns. Do you recall the anecdote about my own garage sale? Well, here's a revelation that I waited until now to share with you. Antique dealers are

Use your imagination to get more antiques for your bucks. These 1940s smoking stands (now considered taboo for their original use) would make great plant stands.

(Author's collection)

some of the biggest fans of garage sales, flea markets, and thrift stores. Most of them probably don't want to admit it, but they regularly scout these places for their merchandise. I applaud their practice because they're right on target. Once, at a show I discovered an item from my garage sale in a dealer's display, which proves, as I indicated earlier, that antiquing is one of the oldest forms of recycling.

FLEA MARKETS: FOR ANTIQUERS ITCHING FOR A DEAL

The second type of sale, known as a flea market, is equally common and is conducted by multiple sellers, usually in parking lots or fields. Don't let anyone try to convince you that you can only find junk at flea markets. Your best chance for hitting the antiques jackpot is at these marketplaces. These mobile forms of merchandising are currently so popular that more than five thousand flea markets are regularly held in the United States in just a single year.

. . . .

Don't let anyone tell you that you will only find junk at flea markets; these are the best places to hit the antiques jackpot.

. . . .

American flea markets are based on the original French open-air outlet, the Marché aux Puces, which opened in the 1860s. Its name literally means "market of fleas." Several theories exist to explain how the Parisian center got its name, but the most logical suggests that those who disapproved of the second-hand goods sold there coined the name as an insult. The derogatory name implied that the used, upholstered furniture was so shoddy that it was infested with fleas. The title stuck but, ironically, the term that was once filled with contempt gradually gained a more positive connotation and became accepted by antiquers on both sides of the Atlantic.

To better grasp the immense appeal of flea markets, skim through the *Maine Antique Digest*, which is the final authority for many veteran antiquers. You'll find ads from the Rose Bowl Flea Market in Pasadena, California; the Philly Antique Flea Market in Fort Washington, Pennsylvania; and the Big Flea (my favorite name) in Richmond, Virginia. Check the classified sections of local newspapers listing flea markets and garage sales in your area, and you'll be amazed at the number open on any given weekend, especially during the warmer months.

"Woolworth's" are Retro heaven and often display these rotary telephones.

(Photo courtesy of Middletown Journal)

Flea Markets or Antiques Markets?

This brings up a quirky point about terminology concerning outdoors markets. You may have heard the expression "antiques markets." Managers of outdoor shows often get furious when you call their bazaar a "flea market." When doing my antiques column, a few have corrected me by saying, "It is an outdoors antiques market, not a flea market." What difference does the title really make? After all, both markets sell used merchandise, which is what antiques are. Perhaps show professionals think "antiques market," the preferred British term, sounds ritzier than "flea market" because flea markets are associated with mundane items like tube socks.

Those exhibitors should visit the empress of all flea markets I just told you about, the French original. Those infamous tube socks, so often a flea market specialty, are even peddled in Paris. I have walked through booths around the perimeter of the Marché aux Puces, where those Retro fashion icons can be found. But make no mistake, first-class antiques abound there, too. It's a safe bet that tube socks can be found in British "antiques markets" as well. The name of these informal bazaars really doesn't matter. The important thing is to have a good time when you go. You'll be rewarded with quality merchandise and friendly prices.

. . . .

Antiques malls, unlike flea markets, have knowledgeable employees to do the selling.

. . . .

Old-Fashioned Flea Markets Only

As you drive along highways, you may notice huge flea markets at major exits that are essentially enclosed shopping malls. These emporiums may have bargains galore on new merchandise, but rarely do they have anything remotely antique. Most true antiques dealers don't set up anymore at these places because the antiques mall phenomenon has changed the nature of the business. It's now easier for them to sell in malls that specialize in antiques. Antiques malls, unlike flea markets, have knowledgeable employees to do the selling. This frees time for dealers to scout for more merchandise, which according to most, gets tougher all the time.

Shopping under a big tent adds old-fashioned pizzazz to an outdoor show.

(Photo courtesy of Queen City Shows)

Vintage women's clothing, called "textiles" in antiquese, is usually plentiful at outdoor shows.

(Author's collection)

above: Blond furniture from the 1940s has really caught on but remains affordable at flea or outdoor markets.

(Author's collection)

left: Here's another example of semi-antique/collectibles awaiting you at "Woolworth's."

(Photo courtesy of Middletown Journal)

When you're on a trip and see one of those grandiose flea markets, keep driving. If nature and your gas tank cooperate, hold out until you see a billboard advertising an antiques mall or shop. This will give you a more productive rest stop. For our purposes, the best flea markets are the informal ones found in parking lots on weekends. It has been my experience that these open-air forums are the most likely to hold hidden gems, so they offer the best opportunity for finding true values in antiques.

Chairs like these are usually great deals.

(Author's collection)

SALVATION ARMY AND GOODWILL STORES

Like garage sales and flea markets, Goodwill and Salvation Army stores have been around for ages and provide excellent antiquing potential. Quality goods and great buys routinely appear at thrift stores thanks to donors who are generous or unaware of the value of their gifts.

Here's a prime illustration of being at the right place at the right time. Back in the 1970s, I purchased an item at my local Goodwill store just before it became chic. I bought the 1920s oak kitchen cabinet for $75. I literally snatched it up as it was being put on display. A few years later, that semi-antique/collectible became a prize for collectors, which inflated its value to about $250. It's too bad I no longer have it because its current retail price is about ten times its 1970s cost, or about $750. Trendiness increases prices, but we have to let go of our jewels when we outgrow them or when clutter takes control in our homes. (More about this later).

Prices at Goodwill and Salvation Army stores are clearly posted and are usually firm. If you feel especially sportive, test your negotiating skills on the manager to try to get a better price. You might get results, or at the very least, you'll get more experience at being an antiques jock.

Aluminum tables and chairs are once again fashionable, and the 1940s version
still remains affordable at many informal markets.

(Author's collection)

Timing for New Merchandise

Cruise thrift stores regularly to learn when new merchandise is delivered. Arrange your schedule to be present when the trucks are unloaded so you get first shot at sleuthing for any underpriced treasures. Many thrift stores post signs requesting donors to drop off items on certain days. If this is the case at a store you visit, be sure to get there the next morning.

RUMMAGE SALES

Churches and civic organizations frequently run second-hand thrift shops and sales near churches or schools. They may only be open a few days a week, but you can find wonderful bargains at these places. Check neighborhood newspapers for hours, etc.

Glassware like these 1940s semi-antiques/collectibles can often be purchased at "Woolworth's" for under $10. Don't forget to bring bubble wrap.

(Author's collection)

Museum Quality?

The Cincinnati Art Museum used to conduct top-drawer sales to help cover operating costs. "The Big Sale" conducted in the Cincinnati Convention Center was more like the old-fashioned rummage sales the British call rumble sales. Donated items included everything from draperies to sofas and antiques.

When guests compliment my currently fashionable red-and-white "Vista" pattern china, I love to say, "Thank you. It came from the Cincinnati Art Museum." Then I set the record straight by adding, "from its big rummage sale." I take great pride in knowing that I only paid $25 for this beautiful set, which shows the potential of shopping at these types of sales.

Still Bargains Galore

To find good stuff at these various marts, you may have to sift through a lot of riffraff, but you'll find it worth the effort. The treasures you unearth will probably have down-to-earth prices because they are antiques-to-be.

. . . .

The treasures you unearth at rummage sales will probably have down-to-earth prices because they are antiques-to-be.

. . . .

It was certainly that way back in the 1970s, when Roseville, Weller, and McCoy pottery regularly appeared at these places. These now highly collected Ohio ceramics dating from the 1930s through the 1950s could be bought at these informal marts for almost nothing. Prices back then started at about $5 and went no higher than $25 to $35 for most.

During the last two decades of the twentieth century, vases, baskets, and bookends crafted by these Ohio potters have become quite stylish. This new lofty status of being antiques-shop merchandise has inflated prices to the upper hundreds or more for most pieces. And special items like big flowerpots on pedestals (jardinières on stands) can sell for thousands. The door for finding reasonably priced pottery has pretty well been slammed shut. But don't get discouraged because later I'll show you how to find more affordable examples of these beloved ceramics.

Rocking chairs are one of the best deals in antique furniture, especially at "Woolworth's."

(Author's collection)

Like many of us, people selling at these marts probably watch television programs about antiques. These shows make them alert to what they are offering, and may lead them to overestimate the value of their goods. This makes it all the more difficult to spot the "Rosevilles" and "Wellers" of today and get them for a song. But there are still ways to find valuable pieces at bargain prices.

The Prepared Antiquer

The antiques jock, like other athletes, must have the right equipment to win. To make your game easier, I would like to recommend two antiquing accessories to have with you wherever you shop.

1940s upholstered pieces can be downright steals at "Woolworth's."
(Author's collection)

- -

To be an antiques jock, use the right equipment:
bring a cloth bag and bubble wrap,
and wear comfortable shoes.

- -

Bag It

Always bring a cloth shopping bag along on your excursions to carry what dealers call "smalls." Just because we're hitting "Woolworth's" doesn't mean we can't have an uptown air (to go with our prosperous attire). So choose a good-looking carrier that will make you proud. (My niece and her husband just gave me a spiffy one from Marshall Field's that's now my official antiquing bag.) These sacks are perfect for little antiques such as china, candlesticks, or anything else that they can hold. Also be sure to have bubble wrap in your sack to protect fragile items. These little conveniences keep you from worrying about splitting bags or chipping china, and allow you to focus on antiquing.

Lamps turn up at "Woolworth's." Just be sure to rewire them.

(Author's collection)

If the Shoe Fits...

Every serious antiquer should always wear a pair of comfortable, quality walking shoes. Antiquing requires a lot of exercise. Whether at shows, flea markets, or shops, if you want to see all the antiques on display, you have to walk! This healthful perk will benefit your physical and mental well being just like any other workout, but to fully enjoy it, you need to keep your feet and legs from getting sore.

SAVVY STRATEGIES
Early and Late Birds Catch the Antiques

If you want to snatch up bargains at "Woolworth's," arrive early. Also, if you have time, return just before closing for one final peek. By being an early bird, you might spot an unappreciated treasure, and by returning late, you might get something at a greatly reduced price when the seller is tired and eager to quit. We'll cover more of this crucial subject in Chapter 10.

A Final Bonus

Remember that I said antiques hold their value? To illustrate that point, I told you how I sold a six-month-old sofa for a tenth of its new price. That sad experience reveals another perk antiques brings to our lives. While looking for antiques at informal outlets, check out everything, including just plain old used stuff. You just never know what inexpensive items you'll find that will prove useful.

You can find second-hand items such as pots, garden hoses, and sofas for your home costing practically nothing compared to new items. I once bought a pair of garden urns for my front porch at a garage sale for five dollars. They still look as if they came from the wonderful garden store Smith & Hawken.

9

Snookering-Free Antiquing for Major Purchases

REPUTABLE DEALERS + GETTING IT IN WRITING = SAFE ANTIQUING FOR MAJOR PURCHASES

Chapter 7 taught you how to bargain for antiques, and in Chapter 8, you learned how to shop at "Woolworth's." The time has arrived to purchase major antiques. I can fully understand why this might make you nervous. Much of your money could be involved, and you might be concerned that an antique is fake or not nearly as old as the seller claims.

. . . .

Shopping for more expensive antiques might make you nervous. Fortunately, there are ways to keep this process safe and stress-free.

. . . .

Fortunately, there are ways to keep your shopping for more expensive antiques safe and stress-free. First, continue using Sensual Testing for Safe Antiquing. This tactic works just as effectively at shows and shops as it does at "Woolworth's." Second, because more of your money could be involved, you'll need to follow additional safeguards. I want you to be able to shop worry free so you can have a really good time. Let's first discuss places to avoid and then venues where you can buy with complete confidence.

Places to Avoid

When it comes to shopping for heavy-duty antiques (for us, that's anything that costs more than $35), stay clear of certain types of establishments. Avoiding them will help you avoid potential costly and embarrassing mistakes.

Crafts Are Great for Crafts, But…

Whenever I see a billboard advertising an antiques shop, my first impulse is to stop. But if the sign also mentions crafts, I keep going. Although crafts shops are fine, it is better to skip these places if you're looking for antiques. Such stores are great for the do-it-yourself person, but few have genuine antiques.

Only Window Shop at Tourists Areas

When on vacation, limit yourself to window-shopping at antiques shops located in high-tourist areas. Places catering to travelers tend to inflate their prices and offer very little authentic merchandise among their colorful souvenirs. Of course, not all places geared for tourists are second-rate. In Charleston, South Carolina, for example, I have had numerous, cheerful excursions eyeing the many high-end antiques shops on marvelous King Street. Just be aware that fashionable areas typically cater to wealthy vacationers.

The Perfume/Potpourri Rule

A student in one of my antiques classes offered a wise piece of advice. She said that if a shop smells too much like perfume or potpourri, she promptly leaves. She believes that means the store emphasizes gifty items rather than antiques. While sweet smells are pleasant, they are no substitute for quality antiques.

The wonderful Galerie Mazarini in Lyon, France, where buying antique art is a safe adventure.

(Photo by author)

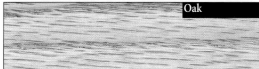

Rocking chairs are great buys, and this early 1800s example—which is even labeled—has a pre-auction estimate of $300-$500.

(Photo courtesy of Skinner's Auction Company)

The samples above show the grains and colors of popular woods. *(Photo courtesy of Howard's Wood Products.)*

Can you tell if this antique china is in less than mint condition? I shall never tell.

(Photo courtesy of Garth's Auctions, Inc.)

Blue and white English Staffordshire from the early 1800s is very expensive, but Chapter 15 outlines ways to snag affordable pieces. *(Photo courtesy of Skinner's Auction Company)*

Here's the china that started the great love for blue and white porcelain made in Canton. This china from China came only in this celestial combination and is the inspiration for the "Willow" pattern. See Chapter 15 for ways to afford Canton. *(Photo courtesy of Skinner's Auction Company)*

Old magazines are full of practical information. I learned that my round white Wedgwood covered bowl, like the one in the left center of this picture from a 1968 issue of *Gourmet* magazine, was called an Orange bowl. *(Author's collection)*

"Woolworth's" are known as treasure troves for crocks and stoneware jugs and jars.

(Photo courtesy of Skinner's Auction Company)

Visit museum, auction, and dealer displays of first-class antiques such as Chinese porcelain to fully grasp the inferior quality of reproductions.

(Photo courtesy of Skinner's Auction Co.)

This early 1800s Southern secretary desk is a mixture of cherry, maple, and mahogany.

(Photo courtesy of Garth's Auctions, Inc.)

This English pine corner cupboard was originally built-in and probably had received many coats of paint until it was refinished.

(Photo courtesy of Garth's Auctions, Inc.)

This beautiful early 1800s corner cupboard has sadly been painted white over its originally varnished finish. It should be refinished to "look as good as old."

(Photo courtesy of Garth's Auctions, Inc.)

Rub your fingers ever so gently over the curvy cabriole leg of this circa 1770 table, and you will fully relish the detailing involved in hand carving.

(Photo courtesy of Skinner's Auction Company)

When a piece of furniture has replaced handles, as does this 1770 maple highboy/tall chest, that's good news for budget collectors.

(Photo courtesy of Skinner's Auction Company)

Auburnish mahogany beautifies this bracket clock created in London about 1800.

(Photo courtesy of Skinner's Auction Company of Boston)

Keeping a flexible shopping list and sitting through a whole auction may net you a bargain such as these miniature portraits. *(Photo courtesy of Garth's Auctions, Inc.)*

Auction catalogues provide a feast for your senses. Just look at these hooked rugs, pewter pieces, and Windsor chairs.

(Photo courtesy of Skinner's Auction Company)

Here's another example of how semi-antiques/collectibles can stretch your purchasing power. Instead of purchasing silhouettes from the early 1800s, buy 1930s reproductions, which look almost as authentic as these genuine examples.

(Photo courtesy of Garth's Auctions, Inc.)

It's fun to learn by looking at these wonderful, upscale coverlets and quilts dating from the 1800s.

(Photo courtesy of Skinner's)

These beautiful terrestrial and celestial globes, originally for a stately English library, are reminders to avoid pairs.

(Photo courtesy of Skinner's Auction Company)

By giving a young "computer junkie" a vintage microscope, you may just have created a future antiquer.

(Photo courtesy of Skinner's Auction Company)

This sewing desk made in New Hampshire in the 1860s has a double sensuality because it makes us want to touch and read its provenance. *(Photo courtesy of Skinner's Auction Company)*

A superb William and Mary lowboy, or dressing table, from 1710 falls under the traditional pre-1820 definition of antique.

(Photo courtesy of Skinner's Auction Company)

Notice the veneer on the drawers fronts of this circa 1797 sideboard from Annapolis, Maryland.

(Photo courtesy of Skinner's Auction Company)

The Sensual Approach asserts that usually the heavier a piece of furniture is, the better its quality, which is the case with this 1830s cherry chest. *(Photo courtesy of Skinner's Auction Company)*

Doesn't looking at this mid- to late-1700s walnut chest of drawers from France make you want to caress its carving?

(Photo courtesy of Skinner's Auction Company)

Mary Robertson ("Grandma") Moses (1860-1961) is perhaps the most famous Naïve Art painter. Her painting *Old Mill on Sunday* had a pre-auction estimate of $25, 000 to $35,000. Plenty of pictures by naïve artists are still available for less than $200. *(Photo courtesy of Skinner's Auction Co.)*

A rather recent limited edition print by Calder is an example of a future antique.

(Photo courtesy of Garth's Auctions, Inc.)

This lovely scene by British artist George Smith (1829-1901) is worth many thousands, but there are ways to acquire gorgeous but far less costly pictures.

(Photo courtesy of Skinner's Auction Company)

Mother Nature loves antiques because collecting antiques saves trees from being destroyed, as depicted in this logging scene by V. Casinelli (1868-1961).

(Photo courtesy of Garth's Auctions, Inc.)

left
This Italian plaque from the late 1800s shows us that Victorians often had romance on their minds.

(Photo courtesy of Skinner's Auction Company)

Paintings of flowers such as these by Laura Coombs Hills (U.S.A. 1859-1952) follow the Feng Shui philosophy of positive energy.

(Photo courtesy of Skinner's Auction Company)

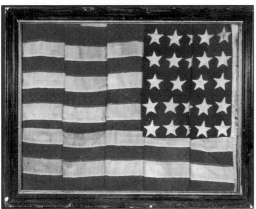

This Civil War flag has quite a provenance, which of course means its winning bidder paid dearly for it.

(Photo courtesy of Skinner's)

Visiting museums offers nonstop learning opportunities. This watercolor by Henry Walton (U.S.A., active 1836-1850) offers a terrific insight into home decorating of the 1840s.

(Photo courtesy of Skinner's Auction Company)

When traveling, always visit local museums such as New York's Metropolitan Museum of Art.

(Author's collection)

A $65,000 Tiffany lamp is grand, but many more affordable antiques are out there waiting for you.

(Photo courtesy of Skinner's Auction Company)

These Native American beaded-hide moccasins crafted in the 1800s are a truly American antique to collect.

(Photo courtesy of Skinner's Auction Company)

Sometimes there seems to be no logical reason why a choice late-1700s sofa might go for a song at auction. Just stay to the end to hopefully snag a sleeper.

(Photo courtesy of Skinner's Auction Company)

This walnut circa 1760 Queen Anne chair was crafted in Newport, Rhode Island.

(Photo courtesy of Skinner's Auction Company)

The 1700s mirror with eagle sold for about six times more than its younger cousin. *(Photos courtesy of Garth's Auctions, Inc. and Skinner's Auction Company)*

Gut Feelings

As a disciple of Sensual Testing for Safe Antiquing, always trust your emotional response. If you get bad vibes in a shop or mall, leave. But if you experience a sense of peace and well being, stay and enjoy. Follow your intuition; it will always give you an accurate reading.

. . . .

Relying on your instincts is an excellent way to find reputable dealers. But if you prefer outside help, turn to a computer or word of mouth.

. . . .

Not too long ago, while strolling through the beautiful French city of Lyon, I discovered an exceptional art gallery. Upon entering Galerie Mazarini, my instincts identified it as a place where I could buy with confidence. The owner, Madame Riva, supplied fascinating information about the artist of each painting, and offered very fair prices. My successive visits, and especially my most recent excursion, which included Dianne and Pete, have been so satisfying that all three of us now jokingly call our houses "the American Branches of the Galerie Mazarini." Wishing I had more wall space is a wonderful problem to have. You will, no doubt, eventually face the same dilemma, so later in the book I offer profitable solutions to this unexpected yet pleasant challenge.

Relying on your senses/instincts is an excellent way to find reputable dealers. But if you prefer outside help, turn to a computer or, my favorite tool, the foolproof, old-fashioned word of mouth.

Word of Mouth

Computer research, as a first step, is a fast way to identify the location of malls and shops in your area. When doing research, you'll probably find retailers with glitzy Web pages listing endless credentials. However, I prefer a more tradition-

A brochure supplied by the very reputable Galerie Mazarini in Lyon, France.

(Author's collection)

al way of finding exemplary dealers. Even though the Internet can instantly provide massive amounts of data, word-of-mouth recommendations still provide the most reliable information about dealers.

Ask your collecting friends which dealers or estate sales conductors they prefer. They will share names of honest, knowledgeable, and fair dealers. And they'll also warn you about sellers who can't be trusted.

When you enter an antiques emporium or an estate sale endorsed by someone you know, make sure you pay attention to your first impressions. As I just said, your gut reactions won't deceive you. If your heart and mind are pleased, start meandering. As you look around, check for detailed descriptions of the merchandise, which you now know are definite indicators of a quality seller. That's just what Madame Riva and so many other top-drawer pros do in their own businesses. Now let's take a brief look at antiquers' collecting styles.

A 1937 advertisement for antiques from a very reputable antiques dealer.

(Photo courtesy of Antiques Magazine)

Spontaneous Antiquer or Methodical Antiquer?

Are you a spontaneous collector? When you spot a gem at the right price (regardless of the fact you have no idea where you will put it in your home), do you simply have to have it? Or are you a methodical antiquer on a mission looking for certain items? If you're methodical, your shopping list is always in hand, and you look only for specific antiques, such as a table for the living room or a mirror for the bedroom.

Comparison Shopping

Sensual Testing for Safe Antiquing works well for both shopping styles. But be aware that both types must do some homework to be successful. Methodical collectors should do theirs before they go antiquing, while spontaneous buyers should research after they spot their desired item. A little work can save you from getting a royal snookering and provide an opportunity to pat yourself on the back for having spotted a terrific deal. Fortunately, there is nothing to the groundwork.

Compare your assignment to shopping for clothes. When you find shoes at Lord & Taylor, you want to make sure you get the best possible price. By researching the brand name on the Web, you'll be able to create a list of other stores handling the same footgear. You'll probably also find online catalogues showing competitor's prices. This will give you the information to determine whether you think Lord & Taylor's prices are reasonable or inflated. You can use the same course of action for comparison shopping for antiques.

. . . .

Both spontaneous and methodical shoppers must do some homework to be successful comparison shoppers. A little work can save an antiquer from getting a royal snookering.

. . . .

Let Your Fingers Do the Walking on the Keyboard

Here is how both spontaneous and organized collectors can research prices for comparable antique grandfather clocks using the computer. Start by typing "grandfather clock," in a search engine on the Web. Or on an Internet auction site such as eBay, enter "grandfather clock" (or the broader term "antique clock"). Gather prices from as many sources as possible to get the most accurate estimate of price trends.

Your research may also turn up other helpful information such as age, style, or origin of grandfather clocks. However, if you can't find similar clocks, (which happens more often than you can imagine) try another time-tested strategy.

Let Your Fingers Do the Walking at the Library

Locate the various price guides that are usually available in the art and music department in your public library. In *Warman's* or other reference books, look in the sections covering clocks.

You should find realistic retail prices (what you should expect to pay in a shop, mall, or show) for similar grandfather clocks.

Let Your Fingers Do the Walking in Person

This strategy for safe antiquing works particularly well in malls or at shows. Because this method is so fast and simple, it will undoubtedly become a reflex every time something appeals to your antiques palate. Imagine that a green 1930s Depression glass bowl priced at $40 at a mall winks at you. Before passing on it or hauling out your checkbook, compare prices at nearby stores. Be like my Gram, who made a living of comparison shopping in the 1920s. As a Marshall Field's employee, she scanned prices at competing department stores in the Chicago area. Malls or stores usually have so much merchandise that it makes it a cinch to check prices for similar items. Comparison shopping can save you from being snookered and give you confidence that you are making a wise purchase.

. . . .

At malls and shows, compare prices at nearby stores before passing on an item or hauling out your checkbook.

. . . .

THE ULTIMATE SAFEGUARD: A GOOD RECEIPT

Before you pay for an item, take a close look at the receipt. Most dealers still provide a handwritten receipt with a description of the item along with the more modern cash register receipt. If the seller is not willing to put this information on the handwritten receipt, then you're smart to pass. Remind yourself that you will find another charmer, perhaps at the next crossroads. When I purchased a small table from Fred Henderson, a Sharpsville, Indiana, dealer, he created the ideal receipt by including the words, "Everything guaranteed [as authentic]."

Here's another example of an honest dealer who stated way back in 1937, "with slight nicks on knob."

(Photo courtesy of Antiques Magazine)

GENTILITY GUARANTEES REWARDS
Favorite Dealers

If you're consistently pleased with a dealer, it's smart business to stick with that dealer. On future purchases, you can be sure you'll receive preferential treatment, which usually includes favorable prices and first pick on choice merchandise. In addition, you will be accumulating more Feng Shui positive energy because you acquired them under pleasant circumstances. My prized highboy I told you about in Chapter 2 means so much more to me because I really like the Browns, who made it possible for me to own the antique of my dreams.

Friendly Prices

After you have established a good relationship with a dealer, you can follow up with a move that combines good manners with smart business acumen. Send a note telling the seller how much you love your antique, and be sure to mention your appreciation of the sweet price.

The next time something whets your antiques whistle with the same dealer, the "bread and butter" letters will pay off. You will probably be offered the best price right off the bat, making negotiation unnecessary. No doubt creating this type of relationship is how the term "friendly price" originated. It's amazing that more of us don't take advantage of this simple, five-minute task.

Layaway

Many professionals at shows, malls, and shops offer layaway. Layaway allows you to budget your money for really special antiques. Just place a deposit and make small payments on a regular basis. When your bill is paid in full, you can take your trophy home. You'll enjoy it all the more knowing that your budget remained intact by paying a little at a time. During my impoverished graduate school days, I relied on this system, which helped me acquire some prime antiques. This plan is so handy that even now I use it from time to time. (This just shows you that some things never change and that I antique as I preach.)

No Credit Card Debts

Sometimes sellers offer a financial arrangement that even beats layaway. As I pointed out earlier, a successful, long-term business relationship between you and a dealer results in mutual trust and friendship. Dealers have been known to offer special payment plans to favored clients to sweeten the appeal for their high-end antiques. Their terms beat credit card purchases because their special plan charges no interest. Sometimes they'll even let you take your antique home before you've even made a single payment. As you can see, sticking with a proven dealer has personal and financial benefits.

LOOMISM

You get what you pay for when you buy from first-class dealers, but you won't necessarily pay full price if you've established a good rapport with them.

10
Timing Is Everything at Shows

THE BEST TIME TO BE AN ANTIQUES JOCK

The last chapter gave you additional tools for safe antiquing. Now the fun part really begins; you're about to become a major league player at antique shows.

Why are antiques shows so worthwhile? First, shows offer a huge selection of choice goods often being shown to the public for the first time by knowledgeable professionals. Second, you get a first-class tutoring session as you scan the information about the antiques. And third, you get an insurance policy—one not usually available at "Woolworth's." As I pointed out earlier, when you buy from a dealer, make sure you get a receipt with a complete, written description of your purchase. The receipt is your guarantee that you won't get a royal snookering. And last, but not least in importance, just attending shows offers a great escape from daily reality.

LOOMISM

At antique shows, if you buy from reputable dealers and get it in writing, you can ignore the $35 Antiques Ceiling.

Several opinions exist concerning the best time to arrive at a show to get the most wonderful deals. Antiquers are constantly debating this point. Many insist that being at the opening is the only way, while others argue that walking in late is far wiser. Also at issue is the question of whether to pay extra for higher-priced "preview" or "early" tickets. These admissions allow you to examine the goods a few hours (or sometimes even a full day) before the general public.

. . . .

Antiques shows are worthwhile because they offer a huge selection of choice goods, and knowledgeable professionals will provide detailed receipts.

. . . .

ARGUMENT ONE: ARRIVING EARLY

Countless experienced antiquers believe that being at the opening is absolutely essential. Why do they feel so strongly about this? It's not surprising that some wait for hours at the entrance to be the first to spot an overlooked treasure, sometimes called a sleeper. What are the odds of finding a sleeper? Your chances are probably better at "Woolworth's." However, one of the really fun aspects of collecting is that you never know what you'll find. Many insist that your chances of discovering diamonds in the rough are much better if you're an early arriver. But another tactic will shortly be revealed that can be equally effective for getting premium antiques at bargain prices.

Some First Arrivers Pay More

Many antiquers are so committed to arriving early that they're willing to pay a premium for the opportunity. Show exhibitors charge collectors who want to arrive early a higher entrance fee. In *Maine Antique Digest*, for instance, the *Concord Antiques Show* advertised a $6 general admission for its noon to 4 p.m. auction. The next line, however, announced a $10 admission for those who wanted to preview the items from 10 a.m. to noon. Antiquers who wanted to find "sleeping beauties" at the Concord show had to be willing to pay 40 percent more to get that chance.

During a February show, The Tailgate Antiques Show in Nashville, Tennessee, charged $5 general admission for the noon opening, but the privilege to sneak in at eight a.m. cost $20, or 400 percent more than general admission.

Preview parties also allow early entrances. These parties are held at posh exhibitions such as the New York City Armory Show, held every year on Park Avenue. At these events, patrons get refreshments and the gratification of reviewing the merchandise before the masses. So there must be something to this early arrival argument if so many are willing to pay more for the opportunity of arriving first.

. . . .

Discerning which sellers are "bedroom dealers" is trickier than it sounds. One clue is that pros usually have more information about their goods than part-timers do.

. . . .

Spotting Sleepers

Most shows are scheduled on weekends so working folks can attend. At such places, you'll find a wide range of dealers and merchandise. Some sellers putter in antiques in their spare time, while others make their living buying and selling.

Collectors who live for spotting sleepers swear that you have to begin early in the day and focus on booths operated by amateurs. It does seem logical that sleepers go hand-in-hand with "bedroom dealers," an affectionate nickname for those who dabble in antiques. But discerning which sellers are bedroom dealers is trickier than it sounds. One clue is that pros usually have more information about their goods than part-timers do.

The numerous television programs about antiques have made most dealers, like the folks at "Woolworth's," more mindful about the value of their goods. You may hear a dealer say, "The same thing was appraised on TV for such and such." A statement like that indicates that you're unlikely to find any sleepers in that display. I doubt you'll find sleepers in any other booths either, as a result of the television shows.

. . . .

If a dealer says, "The same thing was appraised on TV for such and such," you're unlikely to find any sleepers in that display.

. . . .

A Relaxing Early Arrival

If you think you would prefer to arrive early, but want to avoid the stress, try the following game plan. Don't waste precious shopping time trying to find sleepers. Rather, take advantage of your early arrival by casually browsing. Have fun as you shop and learn. When something tickles your fancy, negotiate to get the best deals using the tactics you have acquired in this primer.

Cool Morning Antiquers

If you're naturally an early riser, it seems logical for you to go to outdoor shows in the mornings. By following your internal clock, you have a better shot at finding a pot of gold, and during brutally hot summer months you can shop more comfortably, as mornings are cooler. Don't worry about discovering super finds. Sooner or later, you'll bump into a charmer that will rouse your passions. Those Loomisms for price negotiation will help you net first-class antiques at blue-light-special prices.

ARGUMENT TWO: ARRIVING LATE
Enough Tension During the Week

I personally choose not to be an early arriver. A few unpleasant experiences have convinced me not to arrive at this time. The first hour can be intense while everyone fervently scouts for hidden treasures. This part of the day must be just as difficult for dealers as it is for antiquers. If you feel you can take the turmoil and want to go early, then happy hunting! However, you will rarely see me at any market in the wee hours. If you're like me, you have enough tension in your life during the week. Even though dealers say they make most of their sales right after opening, don't fret. Loads of merchandise will still be waiting for you.

Clocks Favor Late Arrivers

Why do I say there will still be great pickings left and even better chances later on for great buys? It all has to do with clocks. If you were a dealer, would you be willing to come way down in price—especially on your top pieces—in the first minutes of an eight-hour or longer show? Dealers wisely gamble on more shoppers arriving during the rest of the show. That, my fellow antiquers, is the great flaw in the argument supporting early attendance for shows. Experience has proven that dealers become more willing to negotiate at the end of exhibition than at the beginning.

. . . .

*Experience has proven that dealers become
more willing to negotiate at the end of exhibition
than at the beginning.*

. . . .

Where Have All the Shoppers Gone?

As the clock is ticking away, attendance may be dwindling at the show, which makes competition among shoppers less intense. This favorable ingredient for getting lower prices could be the result of a number of factors. The majority of shoppers may be gone by afternoon, or perhaps external conditions may have created a lower-than-normal turnout. The drop in attendance may be due to a local football game, or

perhaps seductive weather has swayed gardeners to work in their yards. In any case, a lack of shoppers (plus some subtleties that may never have occurred to you) can really help your cause. For example, a tired dealer probably dreads repacking, perhaps for the umpteenth time in the last month, the same unsold merchandise. All these factors, plus approaching closing time may sweeten your eleventh hour proposals to dealers who may be more anxious than usual to make sales.

If you see something that whets your antiques whistle, wait until closing time to become the antiques jock.

(Photo courtesy of Sharon Platt/Jennifer Sabin)

Relax and Enjoy

I believe that those antiquers who say that a late arrival is best for deals are correct. I recommend that you arrive soon after lunch and then shop leisurely. Feel free to take time for a coffee break or to chat if you meet friends. As you browse, apply the Sensual Approach to Learning by reading descriptions carefully. Take mental notes or better yet make written ones, and draw a map of the dealers' locations so you can easily retrace your steps. Be sure to ask questions if something perplexes you.

Your leisurely pace also allows you to bring a dog to outdoor shows (if policies permit). As I keep saying, dogs and antiques just seem to go together. Have you ever noticed how many pooches you see at shows? So enjoy yourself and relax. Don't fret about losing antiques to earlier shoppers. If an item hasn't been sold by noon, it will probably still be there when closing time nears.

The Antique Jock Closes In

About an hour or so before the doors are locked, check your mental and written lists to see which of your picks are still available. Now is the prime time for negotiating. Why? As I mentioned before, dealers have little desire and probably even less energy after a long show to haul home their unsold merchandise just to cart it to the next show. By using Loomisms for negotiation at closing time, you'll get such super values that you'll become a dedicated late shopper.

LOOMISM

Arrive at a show shortly after lunch. Take your time to read descriptions and wait until near the end of the show to begin negotiating.

Two-day or Longer Shows

The strategy for two- or three-day shows varies slightly from the one-day-show game plan. Just go during the middle of the last day, and follow the same procedure for one-day shows.

The Last Show of the Season: The Ultimate Fantasy/Reality

Here's the section you've been waiting for, my fellow antiquers! Remember that I mentioned the possibility of getting 50 percent discounts on your antiques? If there were ever a chance of getting such a huge discount, it's at the last show of the season, whether indoors or outdoors.

Be sure to catch the last outdoors show of the warm weather season, which usually runs from April or May through September or October. That means going to the September session of the Brimfield Antiques Show in Massachusetts, which has been a hit with collectors since 1959. Arrive after lunch on the last day of its September session and start scanning the descriptions of the goods.

Who could blame a dealer for getting weary staring at this 1700s chest of drawers if it had not sold after some time?

(Photo courtesy of Skinner's Auction Company)

By waiting until the eleventh hour of the last show, you become the ultimate antiques jock. Your opportunity to get those incredible deals is about to begin. The bargains will be

. . . .

By waiting until the eleventh hour of the last show, you become the ultimate antiques jock. After having looked at the same stuff all season long, dealers are ready to sell their remaining stock, even if it means selling some at a loss. Think of the last show of the season as a clearance sale for antiques. So make these unique circumstances work to your advantage when you negotiate.

. . . .

even more plentiful because dealers don't like to store merchandise over the winter. After having looked at the same stuff all season long, they're ready to get rid of their remaining stock, even if it means selling some of it at a loss. I vividly recall from my own days of owning an antiques shop how demoralizing it was to look at the same items day after day, month after month. That's why stores have clearance sales. Think of the last show of the season as a clearance sale for antiques. So make your bargaining skills and these unique circumstances work to your advantage when you negotiate. Let the dealer make an offer and, with good sense of humor, make a counteroffer. Don't be surprised if you hit a home run in the final exhibition of the year. My antiquing pals and I have taken home gems for half or less of their original price.

During the last session of an outdoors show, I bought 1930s issues of *Life* magazine that were reduced from $5 to $1 each. Being loyal to my antiquing pals, I went to get Dianne and Pete so they could cash in on this incredible deal too. However, when we got back several minutes later, the sixty remaining issues were sold out. "I didn't want to keep them over the winter," the dealer told us. That great buy made a big hit with my nephew as part of his Christmas gifts.

RAINDROPS AND PRICES KEEP FALLING

A forecast for rain or extreme heat can reduce prices much the same way as shopping the last show of the season does. When less hardy collectors shun threatening weather, the unflappable will reap the rewards for their tenacity. As you are now learning, dealers tend to become more amenable to bargaining when fewer shoppers are present. Dedicated shoppers compensate by carrying umbrellas on stormy days and wearing straw hats during a heat wave. And remember that by waiting until closing time for negotiation, the buys can be even more spectacular.

. . . .

Bad weather can reduce prices because dealers are more amenable to bargaining when fewer shoppers are present.

. . . .

My sister and I had one of our best-ever antiquing sessions at a show during a nonstop July rain that left us soaked and shivering, but glowing over our purchases. We chuckled as we were leaving and said how we love storms because our car would not have been so jammed with goodies if it had been sunny.

PROTOCOL AT SHOWS
Kindness to Strollers and Wheelchairs

All of us want to welcome strollers, baby buggies, and wheelchairs at shows. Keep in mind that little tikes, after all, are the antiquers of tomorrow, and wheelchair occupants are just as entitled to the therapeutic effects that come from antiquing as we more mobile antiquers. Whenever I see a fellow antiquer in a wheelchair, I say with a big smile, "There are advantages to everything. Hey, you can keep your goodies on your lap as you move around." This is another example of how antiques are part of the international language of friendship.

No Bulldozers, Please!

There are always a few people who, I presume, are trying to be truly efficient at shows by hauling their loot around in a child's wagon or cart. This works well for larger outdoor lanes, but it gets trickier inside. Even when the aisles are more crowded than Times Square on New Year's Eve, these people bulldoze their way through the throngs. Here's another example of how mighty practical those cloth bags can be for your shopping expeditions. If the hot-rod collectors would follow my advice, their shopping would go even faster, and the rest of us wouldn't have to worry about being run over. Keep in mind that dealers will gladly hold your treasures for pick up later when things are less hectic. Doing away with unnecessary vehicles helps keep narrow lanes antiquer friendly. This makes dealers happier, too; when collectors are free to concentrate on shopping, sales undoubtedly increase.

Some Final Advice

Don't let the controversy about what time to attend shows cause you to miss out on this wonderful pastime. As I have said for the umpteenth time, such extravaganzas should be holidays from daily cares. If you can't go at the times I suggested, don't worry. You'll still find affordable antiques whenever you attend, thanks to your negotiating skills.

11

Buying at Auctions

Buying at Auctions May Net You Wholesale Prices

In this chapter, you'll get yet another exciting and profitable way to nab antiques. In fact, I'll show you how to get buys so incredible they'll seem like wholesale prices. Actually, the prices sometimes are wholesale because many dealers buy merchandise for their shops and booths at auctions. The secret ingredient for this strategy is to think "auction."

. . . .

Prices at auctions are sometimes wholesale because many dealers buy merchandise for their shops and booths at auctions.

. . . .

Clever, alert shoppers who follow the many proposals outlined in this book can find bargains galore at old-fashioned auctions. Traditional (face-to-face) auctions have been in existence for centuries and continue to this day. Now, thanks to the Internet, you can click your way to the traditional auction's high-tech counterpart, the online auction.

Let's review both types of auctions to determine which offers the best values, top selections, and most credibility.

ONLINE AUCTIONS

Everyone seems to be talking about online auctions, where you can bid on practically anything from the comfort of your home. The biggest and most well known Internet auction site is eBay, which Pierre Omidyar founded in his California home in 1995. It has been so successful that in 2001, nearly $9.5 billion dollars in goods in over 18,000 categories were sold. Merchandise included everything from kitchen sinks to ballet shoes. During 2001, the third most popular category for bids was furniture and decorative arts, which of course included antiques.

While antiques are a popular category on eBay, online auctions may not be the best place to buy high-quality antiques.

Oddly enough, when discussing online auctions, I constantly hear dealers touting the high prices they've received, while collectors boast about their bargains. This seems contradictory. How can prices be high and low at the same time? This makes me wonder if the high-tech method is really the best way to buy antiques—at least high-quality antiques.

Two eBay Success Stories

Whether I am teaching, researching an appraisal, or writing books and articles about antiques, I pride myself in my objectivity. So although I have some misgivings about purchasing antiques through Internet auctions, professionalism demands that I present an unbiased review. To get more details about online auctions, I asked my antiquing and writing pal, James Sanford, the film critic for the *Kalamazoo Gazette* in Kalamazoo, Michigan, to tell us about his experiences with eBay.

Jim collects *Oz* books, particularly the titles by Ruth Plumly Thompson from the 1920s and 1930s. After L. Frank Baum, the original author of the Oz series, died in 1919, Ruth Plumly Thompson continued writing a book a year from 1921 to 1939. Jim has taken almost twenty years to assemble a set of first editions. If eBay had existed years earlier, there's little doubt Jim could have built his collection with much less time and effort.

Jim is a big fan of eBay and told me, "I have had really good luck and never had a really bad transaction. Any time I've had a problem, the seller has always come through." His best buy was a copy of *The Cowardly Lion of Oz* published in 1923 that includes twelve color illustrations. He thinks most booksellers would charge at least ten times the $43 he paid. (The appraiser in me took over, and I checked his claim. Jim is absolutely right.) Since Jim is so pleased with his purchases from eBay, I asked his advice to help guide novices. Here's what he said:

"Find the item you're interested in and make a note of the time of the end of the auction. It's silly to bid your maximum amount long before the end of the auction; that will only inflate the price as others get in on it. Using the "Watch This Item" feature is a good idea, because that way eBay will e-mail you shortly before the end of the auction and remind you to bid. Figure out exactly how much you want to spend and don't go over that amount. The last-minute flurry of bids on some items can prompt anxiety that will drive you to spend more than you should. Don't pay more than you feel the item is worth."

Another champion for eBay is my writing mentor, Karen Plunkett-Powell, the author of *Remembering Woolworth's*. She loved telling me about her latest buys, which have included sheet music from the movie, *The Girl From Woolworth's*

(1924), which cost $26. She had been using eBay since it started and found it particularly valuable for tracking down semi-antique/collectible items related to her book research. For illustrations in her book, she had found over fifty vintage items from the defunct five-and-dime chain (whose name we borrowed for our informal antiques marts). Karen had everything from "Evening in Paris" perfume bottles (a big seller at the first Woolworth's) to hard-to-find booklets featuring the Woolworth Building, the store's former headquarters in New York City, for less than $30 each. She couldn't personally visit shops all over America for these items, but she loved to shop the entire country by using eBay.

. . . .

The Diebenkorn affair highlights the danger of buying expensive antiques over the Internet. Online auctions do not permit buyers to practice Sensual Testing for Safe Antiquing, a crucial safeguard for making purchases.

. . . .

A Huge Flop: The Diebenkorn Affair

Jim and Karen consistently have had success with eBay, but another collector suffered a colossal loss on one transaction. In 2001, a bidder paid $135,000 for a painting that was allegedly by renowned American abstract artist Richard Diebenkorn (1922-1993). The seller who bought it at a Berkeley, California, garage sale thought it was genuine, but most experts branded it a fake. The "Diebenkorn Affair" brings up a crucial point I want to make about buying through high-tech markets.

What to Buy with Confidence on the Internet

The key to safe buying from many online auctions is limiting your spending to $35 or less and only purchasing items that offer little or no possibility for debate about authenticity. Jim's

Oz collection and Karen's sheet music are good examples of finding items that are "safe." The authenticity of a book or a piece of sheet music is easy to verify. As you now understand, that involves using Sensual Testing for Safe Antiquing. When your article arrives, give it the once-over with your fingers and other senses to verify that it is genuine.

However, when it comes to paintings, pre-1920s antiques, or rare semi-antiques/collectibles, in which condition, age, quality, and other factors might be debatable, it is wise to follow the $35 rule to be safe. The seller of the so-called "Diebenkorn" was not a gallery owner or professional appraiser or auctioneer. That somber story illustrates my concern about buying through an Internet auction. For major purchases, you are much better off going to reputable professionals. That's the joy and the security of shopping at old-fashioned auctions, shops, shows, or malls, where you can collect substantial pieces with much less risk. But online auctions can be a great source for items other than antiques—including the kitchen sink.

LOOMISM

Limit your purchases to $35
or less on Internet auctions
to be safe.

The Old Way for Auctions is Best

I have another reason for preferring traditional auctions for antiques. They allow me to use the Sensual Approach for Learning and Safe Antiquing, which involves taking my time and escaping daily cares while looking and touching to my heart's content. One of the major drawbacks of online shopping is that it prevents the prospective buyer from using the Sensual Approach.

Shopping online can't even begin to compete with in-person antiquing because no sensuality is involved. Scanning the computer is nothing like stumbling on an antique that takes your breath away. Nor will an online antique give you the

Skinner's information attributes this armchair to the celebrated
1700s cabinetmaker Thomas Chippendale.

(Photo courtesy of Skinner's Auction Company)

opportunity to caress it, give it a good whiff, or try the posterior test.

To me, shopping for antiques via the computer is like buying a tie from an Internet retailer or a mail-order catalogue. There is no sure way to know how it is going to look with my favorite suit until the two are placed together. It is the same with antiques because a digital camera and computer monitor can't capture the rich auburn tones or three-dimensional solidity of an 1830s cherry table. Nor can it bring out the special deep blue embellishing 1900 English china. I don't want to order a tie through catalogues or Internet retailers, and I especially don't want to buy antiques via a computer.

. . . .

Electronic antiquing does not allow shoppers
to experience the rich textures and colors
of antiques, nor does it allow them
to escape home or office.

. . . .

Electronic antiquing doesn't create much chance for escaping daily chores and stress, either. To me, a major weakness of cybernetic shopping is that it keeps you bolted to your computer, whether in your home or office. Shopping from your chair doesn't provide the escapism that accompanies the invigoration of sitting with my fellow antiquers, scanning the goodies, and chuckling as the auctioneer hams it up to get the bids rolling. Your high-tech tour gives you little opportunity to "get happy as we go antiquing," as the Loomis version of the Garland tune goes. Computer shopping lacks this carefree perk that old-fashioned antiquing excursions offer.

Monitors Prevent Personal Contact

The trust and confidence established through eye-to-eye contact between the seller and buyer has little chance to develop in an Internet transaction. Electronic buying leaves practical-

The possibilities of Internet auctions are limitless. Just be sure to buy through reputable houses.

(Photo courtesy of Skinner's Auction Company)

ly zero opportunity to create warm, professional relationships that can lead to friendlier prices in the future.

Remember the tips I mentioned in Chapter 9 for finding reputable dealers? Those techniques may give you more information about an Internet seller, but you'll find it difficult to get a conclusive gut reaction through the limited communication you'll have with a seller over the computer. Unlike shopping in person, high-tech shopping makes the whole process abstract and sterile.

. . . .

On some Internet auction sites, you can shop with complete confidence because they are run by reputable auction houses that guarantee the authenticity of their goods.

. . . .

Reputable Auctions on the Internet

Sometimes, you might be searching for one specific antique that, as Jim pointed out, may take forever via the traditional, more physical and time-consuming method. So it would be foolhardy not to take advantage of the computer when appropriate. The good news is that there are some Internet auction sites where you can shop with complete confidence. When you find a reputable auction house like Skinner's of Boston conducting a sale on the Web, and something appeals to you, go ahead and bid. You're still following the snookering-free formula for safe antiquing because the reputation of the firm and the descriptions of the merchandise guarantee your safety. If you have complete faith in a particular Internet auction house, then feel free to exceed your $35 antiques ceiling. But regardless of how reliable an Internet auction site is, in my opinion, it can't compare with a traditional auction.

A Future Look

I may revise my opinion in the future if conditions warrant, but for now I feel strongly that you should limit computer purchases to $35 or less unless you know the house conducting the Internet auction.

BUYING AT OLD-FASHIONED AUCTIONS

Buying at traditional auctions with a live auctioneer in a gallery complete with audience can offer you stupendous situations for snagging first-class antiques, often at wholesale levels. These prices can be much lower than those at retail shops, malls, and shows.

A good way to understand the concept of wholesale pricing is to study advertisements for used cars. A wholesale price is usually what is listed in the classified sections of newspapers, whereas the retail price is what an automobile agency charges on its lot for a comparable vehicle. It's roughly the same with antiques. Think of wholesale prices for antiques as classified prices and retail prices as what you would pay in most antique shops. Thus, auction prices can be as advantageous to collectors as classified prices are to used-car customers. You are about to see how all this can happen at auctions.

Buying from reputable dealers is a sure-fire recipe for successful antiquing.

(Photo courtesy of Sharon Platt/Jennifer Sabin)

The History Of Auctions

Auctions are known to have existed during the days of the ancient Romans. In seventeenth-century Britain, auctions were usually held in taverns and coffeehouses, and at about this time, catalogues were first used to describe the merchandise. Today, most houses publish these marvelous learning tools for their important auctions. Two famous firms are Sotheby's, which was established in 1744, and Christie's, which was founded in 1766. The rules governing auctions in the 1700s are essentially the same as they are today: the high bidder is the winner.

Madame De Pompadour, Greta Garbo, And Jackie Onassis

When a very prominent person dies, the sale of personal property from the estate usually creates quite a stir among the admirers of the rich and famous, and especially among collectors.

Madame de Pompadour (1721-1764), the mistress of King Louis XV, was a great patron of the arts. Painters and craftsmen loved her because she paid her bills promptly—an unusual practice among aristocrats at that time. La Pompadour, as the French lovingly still call her, especially adored Sevres, the French china whose floral designs have been addictive to collectors for more than two hundred years. Certainly one of the most notable auctions of the 1700s involved the sale of the Marquise's possessions after her untimely death. Her collection was so extensive that it took two months to sell her 2,500 pieces of Sevres. It must have been quite a social coup for the blue bloods to attend her celebrated estate auction.

Here's another example of the pleasurable learning that can be yours by museum hopping when you travel. During a trip to France, your antiques coach attended the stellar presentation "Exhibition Pompadour," which was held at her former part-time residence, the Palace of Versailles outside Paris. Pieces that originally belonged to the Marquise (and sold at her highly touted auction) were accumulated especially for this event from collections all over the world. What an awesome way to get really familiar with out-of-this-world Sevres!

. . . .

Auction catalogues allow you to leisurely browse through items that are about to be auctioned. And you can fax or phone in your bid if you are unable to attend.

. . . .

In the last decade of the twentieth century, the Greta Garbo sale, and of course the Jacqueline Kennedy Onassis auction, created the same public fervor that the Pompadour spectacle had over two centuries earlier. The sales of Garbo's and Jackie's belongings shattered previous auction records. Why were their prices so high? Because of their stellar provenance, which means their history (more about this in Chapter 15).

Catalogues and Estimates

The Pompadour, Garbo, and Jackie auctions verify that this ancient method of buying and selling remains as popular now as it has ever been. When first-class firms such as Skinner's of Boston conduct an auction, try to get a copy of the catalogue. Photos of the merchandise along with important facts are detailed, including age, style, origin, and condition. When the provenance of an item is known, the catalogue includes information about past owners. It's not often, however, that they can boast of legends like La Pompadour, Garbo, or Jackie.

You can buy subscriptions to auction catalogues just as you do for magazines, or you can find out which auction catalogues are now available on the Web. Either way, you can look for merchandise that is about to be auctioned. If something has aroused your interest, you can fax or phone in your bid, or you can bid via the Internet. Just remember that absentee bidding can't compete with the excitement of being in the midst of an audience as the drama unfolds.

Catalogues also present what specialists estimate each item will bring at the auction. The prices are usually given in a low-to-high range, such as $100-$200. These figures are based on what comparable items have previously sold for and are usually an accurate guide to what they will "fetch" (a pet auction term for "bring").

· ·

When you attend an auction, you will absorb a great deal of information from the auction publications and the knowledgeable auctioneers.

· ·

When you attend an auction, especially those accompanied by detailed catalogues, your time is wisely spent. Whether you buy or not, you're following the Sensual Approach to Learning because you're absorbing a great deal of valuable information by reading the auction publications. Moreover, when the auctioneers engage in their sales pitches to arouse interest among bidders, pay attention because they are usually quite knowledgeable.

HOW TO PLAY THE AUCTION GAME
Auction Previews
If at all possible, attend the auction preview so you can closely inspect items in the catalogue that caught your eye. Ask auction specialists about age, quality, condition, origin, and any other information you want to know, so you are fully informed about what you want to bid on. Ask questions discreetly so you aren't announcing your enthusiasm about an item to other buyers. This could increase competition and lead to a bidding war, which means inflated prices.

If, after your questions have been satisfactorily answered, an item still fascinates you, then do some comparison shopping to ensure you bid wisely. Use both the Internet and price guides I mentioned earlier to get a realistic idea of prices.

. . . .

If at all possible, attend the auction preview so you can closely inspect items and ask detailed questions before the bidding begins.

. . . .

The Buyer's Premium

Most auction houses require that you register when you attend their auctions. This is a good time to check the buyer's premium rate and other policies such as payment, storage, and delivery charges. (Also ask about possible extra charges when bidding via the Internet.) A buyer's premium is a percentage added to the winning bid. If you have the highest bid at $100, a fee (usually ranging between 10 and 18 percent) is added. Thus, you end up paying $110 to $118, plus sales tax.

Have you ever watched the British television series *Lovejoy*? The show features an unprincipled antiques dealer, and is based on the book series by Jonathan Gash. It's always a hoot to watch Lovejoy's bidding technique. Trying to be ever so discreet, he slyly winks at the auctioneer because he doesn't want to announce his intent to pursue certain items. Unlike the auctions attended by that rascal, most houses give bidders a small numbered paddle for bidding. That device prevents the classic situation seen in movies and television in which someone's unintentional scratch or cough is misinterpreted as a bid, obligating the person to buy an unwanted item.

Buying with Confidence

You can buy with confidence at reputable auctions because the house stands behind its merchandise, which means you and your checkbook can decide if you want to go over $35.

You can track down good auction houses by following the methods outlined in Chapter 9 for finding reputable dealers.

The Bidding Game

Before you start to do any bidding, write down your top figure for anything that stirs your emotions. Keep that paper handy and go no higher. This is a good way to keep your emotions in check so you don't have to use the overdraft feature in your checking account. Keeping your limit right in front of you will remind you to stay within your bounds and protect your budget.

LOOMISM

Never, never say, "I won." You're paying for what you want. Keep this in mind and you'll keep a level head and won't pay more than you intended.

Jim's earlier advice about not placing eBay bids too soon applies equally to traditional auctions. "Bidding your maximum amount long before the end of the auction will only inflate the price as others get in on it." As Jim suggests, let others start the early bidding and take your time getting into the action. And remember when to quit.

Nail Biting

When you're at an auction, it can be somewhat nerve-wracking (I can't lie to you) as you wait for your prospective antique to come on the block. I like to read or work on my laptop as I wait (and wait and wait). Be sure, though, to keep peeking at the action because you just never know what you might learn from auctioneers or what might pique your interest.

Remaining Genteel

Even if an auction becomes heated, remember to remain sportsmanlike. Because of the competitive nature of an auction, it's especially important to be civil. Avoid getting into a confrontation at all costs. I've witnessed such incidents and can personally attest that they're unpleasant affairs. Another reason to avoid a conflict is that you might end up paying too much. In addition, it's bad for your physical and emotional health. And remember the principle of Feng Shui. What if every time you look at your "trophy," it reminds you of the war you engaged in to win it? The battle will wipe out the positive energy that should have come with it. Keep the competition in

. . . .

When bidding, remember the principle of Feng Shui and keep competition in perspective. Remember that the people in the audience aren't enemies but fellow antiquers.

. . . .

perspective. The people in the audience aren't your enemies but fellow antiquers (whether collectors or dealers), so keep smiling as you bid. Finally, as I keep harping, keep in mind that there are many antiques in the sea of life. If you miss a gem at one auction, don't fret; another is bound to turn up sooner or later. I've endured this many times, and it never ceases to amaze me how soon a similar gem appears on my antiques horizon.

Getting Wholesale Prices

If you doubt you can buy antiques at wholesale prices, take a good look at fellow patrons during your next auction. You'll be able to spot dealers, who intend to buy low and sell high. Look for clientele with very serious demeanors (after all, they are trying to make a living) who are buying large amounts of merchandise. This insight shows why shopping at auctions is a good idea. For your safety net, keep in mind that if they're bidding on what you consider to be out-of-this-world, don't let that sway you to go higher than your written figure.

Keeping a Flexible Shopping List

Keep your shopping list flexible because you just never know when a steal will appear. You may get an item for much less

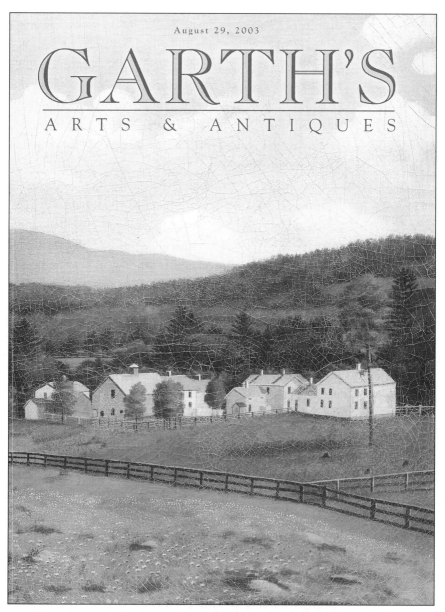

August 29, 2003

GARTH'S
ARTS & ANTIQUES

This is the cover of the catalogue for Garth's Auctions, Inc., located in Delaware, Ohio.

(Photo courtesy of Garth's Auctions, Inc.)

than its pre-auction estimate, which means you could pay a half or third of what you would for a comparable antique in a shop. You have to be "Johnny or Jeannie Antiquer on the spot" and act quickly. That can be challenging, but go ahead and take the plunge into the bidding pool. It's reassuring to know that under such circumstances, you have no concerns about quality because you are attending a sale conducted by a reputable auction firm.

Once, after a two-hour drive to Garth's Auctions in Delaware, Ohio, I was totally frustrated when I lost a delightful small French cabinet. My best figure was topped after only forty seconds of fierce bidding. On a positive note, I congratulated myself for having such a keen eye. I commented, "That piece must be pretty terrific since a dealer catering to the carriage trade ended up paying so much." Then, trying to remain chipper, I said to myself (just as I remind you), "Oh well, there are other antiques in the sea of life," and that's exactly what happened.

LOOMISM

A few items always fail to bring high bids. This usually happens near the end of an auction, probably because both auctioneer and bidders are getting tired and bored. This is a major budget alert.

During the final half hour, a real charmer appeared, and for no apparent reason, I was the only one in the audience who appreciated it. The unesteemed beauty was a walnut English table that was about to go for a third of its pre-auction estimate of $900. Well, I quickly got into the act and nabbed that 1780s tea table for $330 (including the 10 percent buyer's premium). A dealer in a shop would probably ask $1,800 to $2,200 for this understated stunner. It adds so much to my little living room, and until now I couldn't even recall that the French cabinet had been my first choice. That tea table is one of several terrific deals I have bought at auctions by remaining until the very end, revising my shopping list, and thinking very quickly.

Finding "Junque"

Another great opportunity sometimes presents itself. At estate auctions, you'll often see trunks, cabinets, and chests of drawers that contain miscellaneous contents. If you're attending an auction in a home, check the drawers and storage areas before the auction begins to see what's inside. You never know what memento is buried under layers of what appears to be junk. In the last chapter, I'll tell you about a special trophy a friend acquired this way.

Sometimes you'll find odds and ends crammed into bags or boxes. In this case, you should ask what is inside or if you can examine the contents. Whether the bric-a-brac is in a drawer or in a box, you can often get it for almost nothing.

Requesting Receipts

When you pay and pick up your purchase, follow the same procedure as you do in a shop or mall. Be sure to have all pertinent information such as age and origin included on your receipt. If you bought something listed in a catalogue, eventually photocopy its description and attach it to your new-to-you treasure. That way you will always have accurate information for your records and for future owners.

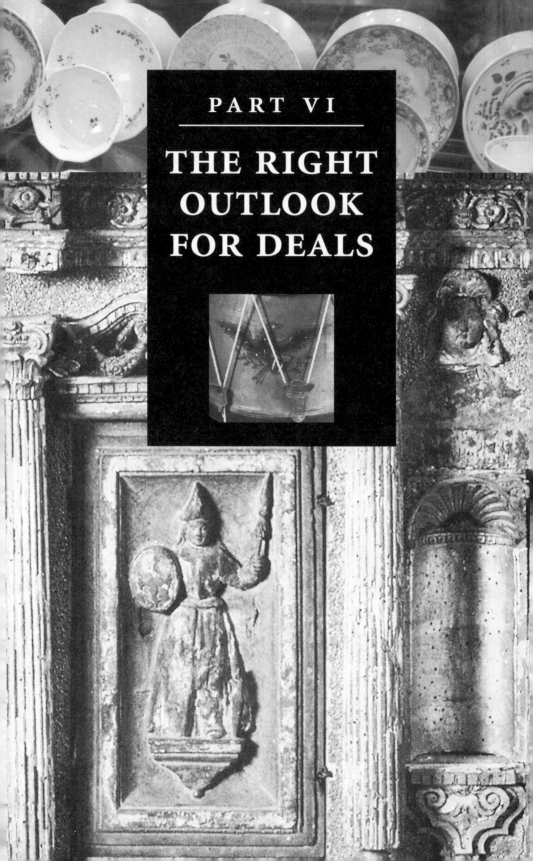

PART VI

THE RIGHT OUTLOOK FOR DEALS

12

Profitable Attitudes

At this point in your antiques journey, I'd like to give you a philosophical pep talk about what I call "profitable attitudes." This training session will explain the attitudes necessary to becoming a shrewd budget antiquer.

ATTITUDE ONE: BE THRIFTY

The first requirement for success demands an appreciation for thriftiness. Clearly, you've already passed this test with straight A's because you're reading this book. And you're probably like

Chapter 12 reveals more ways to acquire upscale antiques such as English Spatterware from the early 1800s by altering your attitudes.

(Photo courtesy of Middletown Journal)

These antique drums from the mid-1800s remind us to collect to the beat of our own antique drummer.

(Photo courtesy of Skinner's Auction Company)

me and wait for a sale before you buy anything that isn't absolutely necessary. If you're especially like me, you avoid paying the asking price whenever possible.

ATTITUDE TWO: COLLECT TO THE BEAT OF YOUR OWN ANTIQUES DRUMMER

People are always asking me, "What's hot in antiques?" My reply (always given with a chuckle) is "Who cares!" Budget antiquers avoid the trendy to get filet mignon antiques at hamburger prices.

When company comes to the Chateau de Loomis (a nickname my friend Rose coined for my little house), I always use my good red-and-white "Vista" pattern English china designed by the Staffordshire potter Charles James Mason. The pattern, set on a white background, portrays a nineteenth-century scene of people walking in a park-like setting. It's an early twentieth-century English version of the famous French Toile fabric that has been around since Marie Antoinette. You see this material on everything now from dog beds to women's slacks.

In the 1980s, the complete service for eight cost me $25. It was such a deal because the pattern wasn't considered hip then. In those days, blue and white ruled as the ultra chic color combination for antique china. Most collectors considered my red-and-white set almost garish, but I didn't care. If the pieces had been in the then-stylish color combination, it would have cost far more than I could have ever afforded. People usually said, "Pink and white, oh my!" No one seemed to notice that the "pink" was actually a deep, almost cranberry/ruby red (a variation of the hue toreadors use for bullfighting).

Collect antiques according to your own tastes, not others', because what is a fashion statement now may quickly become out of vogue, and vice-versa.

Those less-than-favorable reviews of my taste didn't hurt my feelings because I have always collected to the beat of my own antiques drummer. To me, Mason's pattern is perfect, thanks to a special perk. Earlier, I mentioned that certain antiques remind us of loved ones. Vista joyfully does that for me. I cherish this china because my Aunt Panny collected this very same pattern.

Public tastes do change over time, and Vista is now considered quite stylish and is a hit with my guests. What makes an antique an outcast at one moment and a fashion statement at another? For the past several years, I have noticed elaborate presentations of Vista in red and white in many upscale shops and shows, but I rarely, if ever, saw its blue-and-white version. Those stylish displays make me chuckle and say, "Hey, I've always loved it." Then my rapture is replaced by sticker shock because fashion is so costly. Dinner plates now sell for $35 to $45 each. That's almost twice what I paid for the whole thing! Too bad there weren't more pieces at the sale where I got mine.

LOOMISM
To stretch your purchasing power, avoid trendy antiques and only buy what you like.

Italian religious
artifacts from the
late 1400s and
early 1500s are
good buys
because most
collectors prefer
secular antiques.

*(Photo courtesy of
Skinner's Auction
Company)*

My Aunt Panny explained it this way: " 'Everyone to his/her own taste,' said the little old lady who kissed the cow." I have

LOOMISM
There is no such thing as good
taste. It's all subjective.

always suspected she began saying that when she was collecting her own Vista. So buy only what makes you smile, and you'll probably save money and get greater delight by being an independent-minded collector.

I try to follow my aunt's advice, but sometimes the antiques appraiser in me rules. I can't help but ponder what caused the Vista in blue-and-white to drop so much lower in value and chicness than its red-and-white cousin. How do antiques climb the social ladder from garage sale rejects to swanky favorites? By examining their path from fashion outcasts to chic icons, we'll learn more secrets for stretching our antiques dollars.

THE TREND SETTERS IN ANTIQUES

What if we could forecast the next big bang in antiques? That certainly is no easy feat, but I have a few ideas about who gets the antiques ball rolling in setting trends.

Print Media

A few years ago, a decorating magazine displayed a dining room complete with red-and-white Toile wallpaper, matching valences and, of course, red-and-white Vista. It's hard to decide if I should thank the editors or cancel my subscription.

. . . .

*The problem with being on
the cutting edge of chic is
that it costs a lot more.*

. . . .

That article publicly branded my taste as no longer geeky but stylish. That's all very nice, but that's precisely when prices for my china started to skyrocket. It seems the whole world is willing to pay more for Vista than I am. That's the problem with being on the cutting edge of chic; it costs a lot more.

Museum Curators

Another group that can add clout to various antiques is the wonderful gang of museum curators. When a museum show displays certain examples (usually based on artistic merit rather than value), up go the prices for similar types. Newspapers, magazines, and television glorify a show, and those who attend then want similar treasures for their homes. That was the case in the late 1980s when the Metropolitan Museum of Art in New York City presented superb, hand-made American furniture from the late 1800s. The show, titled *The Pursuit of Beauty*, added a great deal of prestige to ultra-ornate furniture that most experts had previously written off as "Victorian curlicue." Now pieces similar to the examples at

In the late 1980s, the Metropolitan Museum of Art in New York City labeled pieces like this "Aesthetic Movement Manner" and, of course, prices soared.

(Photo courtesy of Skinner's Auction Company)

the Met command huge prices, and museums everywhere highlight them in their collections. Unfortunately, museum quality usually means very hefty prices.

. . . .

When a museum show displays certain antiques
(usually based on artistic merit rather than value),
up go the prices for similar types. Newspapers, magazines,
and television glorify a show, and those who attend then
want similar treasures for their homes. Unfortunately,
museum quality usually means very hefty prices.

. . . .

Television

The abundant television shows about antiques have thankfully spread the joy of collecting, but at the same time, they've escalated prices. Check the *Antiques Roadshow* or one of its imitators to see what I mean. For example, not long after a tiny basket was highlighted, similar ones turned up in droves at malls, flea markets, and shops. Prices shot sky high for any little basket that even remotely resembled the television model. Such is the power of television.

My hope is that my own television series, *Is It Antique Yet?*, helped viewers learn about and develop an appreciation for local products. One of my favorite antiques rags-to-riches stories chronicled the success of former slave Henry Boyd. This gentleman became a tycoon in the 1800s because he built beds that didn't break. His design and construction were far superior to that of other manufacturers, whose beds frequently collapsed. I like to think my program played at least a small part in the renewed interest in the pieces crafted by this fine furniture maker.

Those are the primary movers and shakers that create antiques stars. Wise collectors avoid antiques styles that magazines, television, and museums promote.

Attitude Three: You *Can* Let it Go

As you become a more experienced antiquer, you'll eventually face a dilemma that most museums and accomplished collectors encounter: accumulating too much stuff. An important principle of Feng Shui is that clutter is nerve-wracking. As I hinted earlier, the successful antiquer must be able to let go of unneeded pieces to maintain tranquility.

. . . .

An important principle of Feng Shui is that clutter is nerve-wracking. Antiquers must be able to let go of unneeded pieces to maintain tranquility.

. . . .

Museums rarely have sufficient room to display all their holdings. With space at a premium, museum directors have to adopt the de-cluttering procedure known as de-accessioning. When auction houses such as Skinner's, Sotheby's, and Garth's sell pieces from museums, their advertisements proudly tout, "De-accessioned from such and such museum." You can be sure the pedigree of those pieces will bring astronomical prices.

We now face three important questions: When should I de-clutter? How do I de-clutter? And can I, too, profit from my clutter?

When the Time is Ripe for De-cluttering

Thanks to successful antiquing, you'll eventually reach the point when you simply don't have any more room. You'll know when this happens. There are many clues: you stub your toe on an ill-placed chair, you have no more space on your walls or in your cupboards, and your guests have to shimmy their way through your house to get to the dining-room table.

Fortunately, there's a fun and easy way to solve this problem. You don't have to stop collecting. Just upgrade by replacing your current antiques with better pieces. I find it fascinat-

Thanks to the Met's exhibition, ornate, handmade furnishings are now categorized as "Aesthetic Movement."

(Photo courtesy of Skinner's Auction Company)

ing how tastes change as people become more mature and knowledgeable. I won't try to tell you what to upgrade. As I said before, "There's no such thing as good taste. It's all subjective." What one collector considers an upgrade, another may think is a downgrade. You'll just know when it's time to improve your collection.

How to De-clutter—and Profitably, Too!

When you acquire a new piece, make room for it by parting with another. This recycling practice not only gives you more space to properly display your remaining treasures, it allows another collector to share the joy you experienced from a piece. This is probably why auctions, garage sales, and flea

Wait to collect handmade pieces known as "tramp art." They may become more affordable when the fervor over them wanes.

(Photo courtesy of Skinner's Auction Company)

This sideboard is rapidly becoming ready for some de-cluttering.

(Photo courtesy of Skinner's Auction Company)

markets were invented in the first place, so try a sale. You can hold an informal market at your house on a weekend or set up at a flea market. Not only will you clear some room, but you'll also earn cash for your upgrading budget and have the pleasure of meeting the antique's new owner.

At my one and only garage sale that I keep mentioning, I sold a 1910ish armchair to a British lady named Brenda, who is a Cincinnati tour guide. Since we first met on that driveway, our paths have happily crossed again when I've given lectures to her convention groups. It's always delightful to hear (in her charming British accent) how much that chair pleases her.

PART VII

LOOMISMS
FOR DEALS

13

Almost Hall-of-Fame Antiques

AFFORDABLE VERSIONS OF CLASSICS SAVE YOU BUNDLES

With clever shopping, you can match the style and clout of fashionable antiques by choosing more economical versions. I call the antiques that have withstood the test of time "the classics." These elite, eternal stars in the world of antiques are always in demand. Think of the classics as "hall-of-fame" antiques. Of course, by now you have learned that this elevat-

Your antiques coach is crazy about Wedgwood, but china by other English makers may be more affordable.

(Photo courtesy of Skinner's Auction Company)

ed status greatly increases their value. Fortunately, they have more affordable cousins with similar panache but friendlier prices. This terrific group of antiques deserves to be acknowledged, so here are a few examples of "almost hall-of-fame" antiques. I have presented my personal favorites, but there are many more. The following examples will help you spot other versions of "almost hall-of-fame" antiques.

Don't discount the great value that religious art offers! Lady of Guadelupe, a Mexican piece from the 1700s, had a pre-auction estimate of $700 to $900.

(Photo courtesy of Skinner's Auction Company)

Here's a plainer version of Stangl Pottery.

(Photo courtesy of Skinner's Auction Company)

If Rookwood appeals to you, try more affordable pottery by Roseville, Weller, or McCoy.

(Photo courtesy of Skinner's Auction Company)

Ah! "Willow" pattern in blue and white. Other colors such as brown, yellow, and lavender usually cost less.

(Photo by author)

1940s copies of 1700s styles, like these walnut veneered tables, are still affordable.

(Author's collection)

Hall-of-fame antiques have more affordable cousins with similar panache but friendlier prices.

The Hall-of-Fame Antique: Cranberry Glass

Ruby and cranberry are the most charismatic and expensive colors in antique glass.

(Photo courtesy of Skinner's Auction Company)

Collectors of antique glass generally prefer cranberry hues to other colors, such as green and yellow. This favored status gives cranberry glass heftier prices than others. The finest cranberry glass was crafted from about 1875 to 1900 in the Bohemia region of the Czech Republic. Vintage Bohemian decanters in that regal shade can sell for $450 or more. If you've ever seen the sun shining through this wondrous glass, it's easy to understand why it's so cherished.

The Affordable Version: Souvenir Ruby Glass

I assure you that the sun shines just as radiantly through cranberry's next-of-kin, which fortunately is more affordable. Ruby glass was first manufactured in the late 1880s by several firms around Pittsburgh, Pennsylvania. Although this mass-produced glass resembles its Bohemian cousin, it was popularly priced. Even today as a genuine antique, this graceful reminder of bygone days thankfully remains a great buy.

I call ruby glass "the carefree antique" because it was mainly used for souvenirs. In the late 1800s and early 1900s, travelers often had their names, and the dates and places they visited marked on a pitcher, tumbler, or toothpick holder. As the years rolled by, these nostalgic glass pieces became cherished tokens memorializing holidays spent frolicking along the shore or taking in the wonder of World's Fairs.

When I was a young collector, Gram gave me a small cream pitcher inscribed "World's Fair 1893." So my very first antique was a souvenir from the Columbian Exposition, which was celebrated in my beloved Hyde Park neighborhood in Chicago. My debut antique and Vista china add much cranberry/ruby gusto to my dining room, whose color scheme was planned around these two antiques.

Ruby glass souvenirs can be found quite easily. My latest purchase, a large water goblet with the word "Cincinnati"

This happy-go-lucky ruby glass awaits you.

(Photo courtesy of Middletown Journal)

inscribed on its front, rests nicely beside my Chicago pitcher. Even I was amazed at the low price of $22. Besides downright chummy prices, ruby glass has two marvelous perks. First, you'll rarely have to guess their age because most pieces are dated (like my Chicago pitcher), and second, because they're typically souvenirs, you inherit their carefree history.

Your Antiques Ceiling for ruby glass: $45

The Hall of Fame Antique: Quilts

Folk Art, which the British and French so appropriately call "Naïve Art," is special because it's "from the hearts and the hands of the people." That's how Electra Havemeyer Webb (1888-1960), the founder of the Shelburne Museum in Shelburne, Vermont, characterized the artifacts crafted by informally trained or self-taught artists. Her exceptional collection contained paintings, furniture, ceramics, and textiles, which of course included quilts.

· ·

Many pieces of Folk Art are now found in museums and are exorbitantly priced. But, fortunately, more affordable versions are available.

· ·

In the old days, frugal housewives saved every scrap of fabric to be used for quilt making. They created designs using the appliqué method of applying bits of fabric to a background material or by sewing small pieces of cloth into a patchwork. Then they joined the design to a filler and background fabric with small stitching called quilting. The time-consuming methods are the same today as they were in the 1700s. But by 1900, the widespread use of sewing machines made the job easier. These colorful fabric pictures featured flowers, geometric designs, and other motifs that brightened spirits and warmed souls during frosty winter nights in the days before modern furnaces. Their beauty and practicality justifiably guaranteed that they would become family heirlooms.

Quilts boast as many patterns as stars in the sky. Designs include potted tulips on a white background and the classic series of multi-colored concentric circles called the "Wedding Ring" pattern. Fine quality 1800s quilts that approximately fit a full bed routinely garner a pre-auction estimate of $800 to $1,200. That means you can count on a retail price of $2,000 or more in a shop.

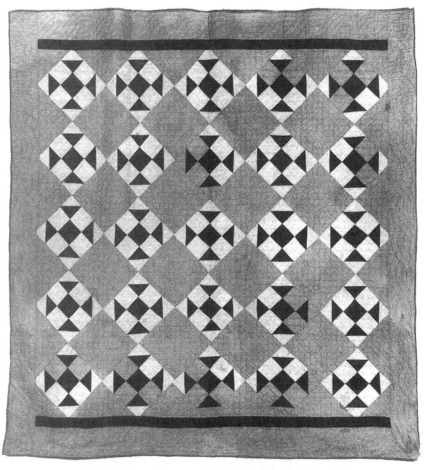

An early 1900s quilt has a pre-auction estimate of $300 to $500, which is much less than an 1800s version.

(Photo courtesy of Skinner's Auction Company)

The Affordable Version:
1930s Through 1950s Quilts

To get more quilt for your money, think younger. Choose semi-antique/collectible examples that feature the designs and craftsmanship of older quilts. Whenever you go antiquing, you can usually find a few stunning quilts dating from the 1930s through the 1950s. Although created by more recent naïve artists, these beauties nevertheless come with the same loving sentiments as earlier ones. But you also get lower prices; they can often be found for under $300 in shops and malls. If your home has a large empty wall protected from direct sunlight, why not hang a quilt instead of a picture?

YOUR ANTIQUES CEILING FOR 1930S
THROUGH 1950S QUILTS: $300

The Hall of Fame Antique: Samplers

Samplers are another definitive example of Naïve Art. The best, which date from the late 1700s to the 1860s, have always been highly esteemed. Recently though, these works of art have become very high end and often cost as much as a swanky new car.

. . . .

To get more quilt for your money, think younger,
but choose examples that feature the designs
and craftsmanship of older quilts.

. . . .

Before the invention of the sewing machine, young women made samplers to perfect their stitching techniques. This fancy needlework usually recorded family history such as births, deaths, and weddings. Roughly the size of an average breadboard, they also included the date, alphabet, and designs such as birds, flowers, vines, buildings, trees, animals (especially dogs), and flowering borders.

I once appraised the most incredible sampler. It truly was antiques perfection, even more stupendous than those I have seen in museums. Everything about it was stellar, including its original frame, family history, and expert stitches with their vibrantly colored threads. This 1700s masterpiece incorporating the principles of Feng Shui featured children, flowers, and a colonial house. Professional discretion prevents me from disclosing its value. Nevertheless, I can tell you that my clients were thrilled with the price it fetched and took joy knowing that its new owners truly revered it.

The Affordable Version: Needlework Pictures

What type of art has the same Feng Shui positive energy, cheerful scenes, and handmade craftsmanship of upscale samplers but at prices that start under $10? Needlepoint pictures. These articles are one of the best buys these days. No matter

Samplers sell for thousands at auction; so choose later needlepoint pictures instead.

(Photo courtesy of Skinner's Auction Company)

what age, subject matter, or type of thread or stitch they display, they are remarkably affordable. My latest coup, which now brightens my bathroom, depicts colorful day lilies. I purchased it in a nice frame for only $7.50. My highest priced needlework was $25, and it's worth every penny and even more because it turned out to be a double gold mine. The picture portrays historic Colonial Williamsburg, Virginia, and came with an antique 1870s walnut frame.

YOUR ANTIQUES CEILING FOR A
NEEDLEWORK PICTURE:

• Framed: $30
• Unframed: $10

To understand the appeal of cut glass, hold a piece to the light and savor its multi-toned luminosity as the sun's rays shine through it.

The Hall of Fame Antique: Cut Glass

Cut glass has been handmade since the time of Christ. From the late 1800s to the early 1900s, American firms crafted elaborate designs that were literally cut into the glass. To understand its magnetic appeal, hold a piece to the light to savor its multi-toned luminosity as the sun's rays shine through it. These antiques, especially those marked (usually on the bottom) by makers such as Libbey or Waterford are quite costly. A medium-sized bowl usually retails for $350 or more and some bigger and fancier pieces sell for thousands.

The Affordable Version: Molded Glass

If cut glass whets your antiques whistle, molded glass will satisfy your thirst economically. Molded glass is inexpensive mass-produced glass shaped by molds into goblets and other

14

Wizardry for "Fixer-Uppers"

Do-It-Yourselfers Save Money

The knowledge you gained about woods in Chapter 6 will help you find quality antique furniture usually ignored by upscale collectors. To get rock-bottom prices, search for a "fixer-upper," a piece that requires a bit of restoration. You'll be able to buy these tarnished gems at greatly reduced amounts because they aren't in pristine condition. By becom-

To get a rock-bottom price for a piece of furniture, search for a "fixer-upper," an item that requires a bit of restoration.

ing alert, you'll routinely spot these pieces in a wide range of places, from garage sales to elite establishments. How can you locate these finds, and what do you do with them once you get them home? In this chapter, we'll examine two important terms—patina and distressing—and the steps needed to restore antiques to their full potential.

A highly valued trait of old furniture is its original finish. When an antique chair is described as being "in a superb state of preservation," that means it has never been refinished.

This 1800 chair was refinished, which reduces its value to $300 to $500.

(Photo courtesy of Skinner's Auction Company)

What is so wonderful about an original finish? The answer is two-fold: patina and distressing.

Patina Is A Treasure

Antiques are more desirable in their original state, which makes them more costly than those altered by refinishing. Why? It all has to do with patina, a word you will hear often in the antiques world. Patina refers to the build-up of dirt and wax on furniture, which darkens corners, cracks, and carving details. Patina is the characteristic that gives antiques a fabulous worn appearance, which frankly, is one of the main reasons they're so appealing. When wooden pieces are stripped, they lose their patina. It can take another century to fully restore their patina because the natural delicate shading can only develop over time.

. . . .

Patina and distressing are the characteristics that give antiques their fabulous worn appearance, which makes them more costly than those altered by refinishing.

. . . .

No Need To Be Distressed About Distressing

Distressing is another important quality of antique furniture. Distressing is a general term for the normal wear—nicks, scratches, worn areas, and sun-faded spots, etc.—that accumulates through years of everyday use. I call distressing "the kiss of time" because it makes antiques look old in a distinguished way. Study "historic reproductions" in furniture stores to find examples of artificial distressing. You'll see how manufacturers deliberately scar, scratch, and dent their pieces to give them the appearance of genuine antiques. So, there's no reason to shun distressed antiques, because that's the way they should look.

This Canadian cupboard from the late 1700s is beautifully distressed. It took years to wear down its paint near the latches.

(Photo courtesy of Skinner's Auction Company)

LUCY KNOWS BEST

Lucille Ball, the redheaded star of the 1950s show *I Love Lucy*, understood the value of patina and distressing. In one episode, she and her friend, Ethel, were watching movers unload furniture when Lucy made an insightful comment. She said, "Our new neighbor either has beaten-up furniture or antiques." Her comment shows she realized that antiques are supposed to look worn and makes me wonder if she was an

antiquer! Antiques by their very nature are old, so they should look their age rather than appearing freshly assembled from a cardboard box.

Sometimes a piece has become so damaged or tattered (as the British so charmingly say) that its overly distressed condition makes it seem junky to most high-end shoppers. But to us, a piece with nicks and faded spots is an appealing fixer-upper.

Sometimes an antique's finish is seriously deteriorated because it has alligatorized. This condition, also called crazing, develops when a varnished surface dries out, causing it to resemble an alligator's hide. Wood is like skin in that it needs moisture. Exposure to excessive heat or sun can cause wood, whether originally varnished or painted, to become "sunburned" or crazed. Periodic waxing moisturizes wood and helps prevent this condition.

. . . .

Flaws provide budget collectors with unparallel opportunities for bargains. Fortunately, these antiques may only need a little work to restore them to dazzling pieces.

. . . .

What upscale collectors consider a flaw provides budget collectors with unparalleled opportunities for bargains. An alligatorized piece usually costs half or less than its pristine version. Fortunately, all it may need is some tender loving care to restore it to a dazzling antique.

Before I pass along tips that will help you transform your "bargain basement" values into wonderful antiques, I want to share two important tenets about antique furniture.

ONCE VARNISHED, ALWAYS VARNISHED!

Furniture originally varnished to showcase the wood's grain should remain that way. Despite the advice trendy decorating magazines offer, you should never paint or "antique" an orig-

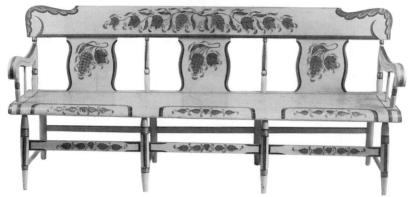

Beautiful painted pieces such as this 1830s Pennsylvania settee should be restored like a painting. Never strip such a piece.

(Photo courtesy of Skinner's Auction Company)

inally varnished object. It's a sin to hide grain and color originally intended to be visible.

Originally Painted Stays Painted

Some furniture in the 1800s was made from pine, the spaghetti of woods. As you may recall from the woods section, in the 1800s, pine was frequently grained with paint to make it look like the costlier mahogany. Sometimes it was decorated with colorful motifs to brighten drab interiors. If you already own a painted piece, then you're lucky because, at the moment, painted furniture is oh-so trendy. If your prize is peeling paint, don't strip it. Stripping will damage its quality and value. Treat it like a fine painting, and let an art restorer preserve it. Since you know that chicness equals priceyness, you probably want to avoid this trendy style when shopping. Instead, focus on originally varnished pieces free from serious structural defects such as a broken leg. Look for items that just need a gentle touch to be reborn.

The Magic Begins

What I especially like about the *Antiques Roadshow* is its emphasis on preserving, whenever possible, the original finish of antique furniture. Why is it smart to avoid refinishing? First, many pieces just need a little effort and a magic concoc-

When the wicker is white, give it another coat of paint. But if the wicker is natural (light brown), leave it alone.

(Photo courtesy of Middletown Journal)

tion to restore them to their grandeur. Second, refinishing must be done very carefully and thoroughly. When you go antiquing, observe how many pieces have been improperly refinished. Poor refinishing jobs exhibit a rough, sandpaper-like finish or a slick, too shiny surface. Poor work like this will make an antique look freshly manufactured. Sometimes your nose will detect a really stinky job. Many times I've been able to smell still-wet varnish at antique-a-thons.

Semi-Fixer Uppers

The following tips are for pieces I call "semi-fixer uppers," which can be rescued without refinishing, thereby protecting most of the patina. Following this section, I'll explain how to refinish pieces that need more extensive work.

. . . .

Why is it smart to avoid refinishing? First, many pieces just need a little effort and a magic concoction to restore them to their grandeur. Second, refinishing must be done very carefully and thoroughly.

. . . .

EPISODE ONE IN THE ART OF TENDER LOVING CARE

After you've purchased a dog-eared antique at a deep discount, you're ready to magically transform it by following my Art of Tender Loving Care. Take your treasure outside and clean it with a rag and Touch of Oranges cleaning formula. This step cleans the finish and gets it ready for the next transforming process. Howard's Restore-A-Finish, which I call the "ultimate miracle worker," is available in nine wood shades to match whatever wood you have. Howard's recipe and my elbow grease have accomplished extraordinary feats. Apply the Restorer liberally on the softest grade of steel wool and rub it in, going with the grain. Wait twenty minutes or longer and then wipe off the remaining liquid with a soft clean cloth. Never use paper towels because they may scratch the surface. Let the piece dry completely.

The final magic involves covering the whole piece in a liberal coating of Howard's Paste Wax, available in similar colors as the Restorer formula. (You can find all these products at antiques malls or online.) Complete your tender loving care by buffing the piece. To make the job far easier, invest in a handy tool called an electric furniture buffer, which looks like a drill with a round, furry disk. Don't wait for a sale because this device is really stupendous. (This extraordinary apparatus came from my friend and restorer of furniture without peer, Allen Gentry, who swears by it.) Your formerly run-down piece, purchased at a greatly reduced price, is once again a handsomely preserved antique. Do try this process; it can produce an incredible renaissance for neglected antique furniture.

If this painted cupboard from 1840, which has really been "kissed by time," seems too tattered, choose less distressed pieces.

(Photo courtesy of Skinner's Auction Company)

A Fresh Look at Paint

Painted furniture can be a financial windfall when you spy a gem whose painted surface hides its original finish. You can usually find sad examples like this for rock-bottom prices

. . . .

You can often find painted furniture at low prices because it requires work to restore it.

. . . .

because few want to take a chance on an antique whose hidden wood is unknown and requires work to restore it. Your wood expertise and the Sensual Testing method will come in handy for determining what possible treasure may be beneath the paint. When you spot a "fixer upper" you think has potential, here's how to tell for sure.

1. Look for places where paint is chipped, revealing wood underneath.
2. Check for areas that have never been painted:
   a. Backs of cabinets, chests of drawers, buffets, etc.
   b. Bottoms of chairs, cabinets, buffets
   c. Backs of legs on chairs, chests of drawers, buffets, etc.
   d. Underneath table tops
   e. Inconspicuous places the painter may have missed

If none of these spots reveal any unpainted wood, ask (always with the honey approach) if you can apply a little paint stripper to expose a small spot in a hidden area.

The Refinishing-Only Option

Sometimes antiques are just too far gone to be rejuvenated by Episode One in the Art of Tender Loving Care. In cases where the finish has become so deeply crazed or has been totally painted, you'll have to refinish the piece. The benefit is that you may have the opportunity to purchase such a keepsake needing revitalization for a third or less of one in mint condition.

You have two options for refinishing. The first is to take the piece to a professional. Furniture restoration is an art and is justifiably costly, so the fee could make the piece more expensive than buying one in good condition. The second option is to do the work yourself, but this will save you a lot of money. I like to call this step Episode Two in our adventures of bringing life back to our antiques.

Episode Two in the Art of Tender Loving Care

In the 1970s, the state-of-the-art (but not so tender) way to remove finishes was to dip pieces into a vat of hot stripper, which quickly removed the layers of paint or varnish. Although it saved time and work, the bath was brutal on antiques. Sometimes glued parts came loose, veneer fell off, or other problems arose. The old-fashioned method of using stripper and a plastic scraper may take more effort, but it's worth the chore. To ensure you do the best possible job, buy only the highest quality paint and varnish remover. Work outside to avoid inhaling fumes, and wear gloves and a surgical mask. After your piece is fully stripped, clean it with mineral spirits and let it dry.

Next, sand very gently using only extra-fine sandpaper and work with the grain. Never ever use medium or coarse sandpaper, which can gouge the wood's surface. Afterwards, wipe the entire piece with a tack cloth to thoroughly remove all dust particles. Then, rub the piece with fine steel wool and apply Howard's Wax in the tint that best matches the wood, again going in the direction of the grain. Give it a thick coat, especially in carved areas like arches on door fronts. Let the piece dry overnight or longer. In time, the shading caused by the dried wax will help replicate lost patina. Complete your restoration by buffing. Use that awesome electric furniture buffer I just told you about, which will prove to

LOOMISM

You'll experience great satisfaction when you restore an antique to its former glory be a fine investment. If you think your piece needs a little more care, wax and buff a second or third time. Congratulations! Pat yourself on the back because your piece is restored without broadcasting that it has been refinished. This heralds a first-class job, which Allen's superb artistry taught me a long time ago. To maintain that lustrous surface, follow the European example of waxing every six months.

YOUR ANTIQUES CEILING FOR PAINTED ANTIQUE FURNITURE THAT WAS ORIGINALLY VARNISHED:

- Bedroom Furniture:
  - Beds:
    Twin: $25 each
    Full: $50
- Chest of drawers: $100
- Chifforobes (combination wardrobe and chest of drawers): $100
- Dressers with mirrors: $100
- Vanities: $50
- Vanity benches: $15
- Wardrobes/armoires: $350
- Living Room Furniture:
  - Bookcases: $100
  - Coffee tables: $25
  - Desks: $50
  - End tables: $35
  - Library/writing tables: $50
  - Secretary desks $125
  - Sofas with exposed wooden frames: $50
- Dining Room and Kitchen Furniture:
  - Chairs: $25 each
  - Servers: $50
  - Sideboards/buffets: $75
  - Tables: $125

Ultimate Buys

Seventeen Loomisms for Deals

This chapter is packed with so many money-saving Loomisms that you can't help but become an even more successful antiquer. I've learned some secrets from working as a professional appraiser, others from experts such as auctioneers and antiques dealers, and several from students attending my classes. Of course, I have picked up a few pointers during my lifetime as a penny-pinching collector on the beer budget I keep mentioning. So get ready for an "antiquer's high," the exhilarating feeling you get when you buy terrific antiques for less than you ever thought possible.

This glorious early 1800s dining room in the Joseph Manigault House in Charleston, South Carolina, has fine mahogany pieces.

(Photo courtesy of Charleston Museum)

This semi-antique/collectible dining suite has that early 1800s styling seen at the Manigault House, but with a more affordable price.

(Author's collection)

LOOMISM ONE
Choose Semi-Antiques/Collectible Versions of Classics

Previously, I explained that antiques made before 1920 are not as common as younger items because they were individually crafted or manufactured in smaller quantities. I also added that many semi-antiques/collectibles were mass-produced, which makes them more plentiful and less costly than their older cousins.

Most antiques establishments offer a wide selection of semi-antiques/collectibles, some of which imitate styles of earlier antiques. A good example is a 1935 reproduction of an 1810 secretary desk complete with glass-front bookcase on top. Both models feature reddish mahogany with a drop-front writing surface and interior cubbyholes—trademarks of this always-in-demand desk that combines good looks with practicality. Would you believe $850 to $950 for the reproduction, versus $8,000 or more for the 1810 model? Hooray for collectibles/semi-antiques! Their affordability makes them all the more pleasing for those of us on limited budgets. They cost much less, yet offer almost the same good looks and quality as their earlier counterparts.

Your Antiques Ceiling for semi-antique/collectible furniture items in reasonably good condition that are just waiting for the tender loving care that I mentioned in the last chapter.

Few can differentiate between the early 1800s mirror and the 1930s/1940s version.

(Photos courtesy of Garth's Auctions, Inc. and Skinner's Auction Company)

BEDROOM FURNITURE

- Beds:
  - *Twin:* $75 (Watch these escalate in value in the next few years because they're becoming chic.)
  - *Full:* $150
- Chest of drawers: $250
- Chifforobes (combination wardrobe and chest of drawers): $250
- Dressers with mirrors: $250
- Vanities: $150
- Vanity benches: $50

LIVING ROOM FURNITURE

- Bookcases: $250
- Coffee tables: $75
- Desks: $250
- End tables: $75
- Library/writing tables/desks: $150
- Secretary desks: $900
- Sofas:
  - If you can live with the upholstery for a few years: $300
  - If immediate reupholstering is needed: $100

DINING ROOM AND KITCHEN FURNITURE

- Chairs: $75 each (only if part of a set of six or eight; see Loomism Twelve)
- Hoosier/kitchen cabinets: $150
- Servers: $150
- Sideboards/buffets: $175
- Tables: $150

LOOMISM TWO
Hang 'em High or From Afar

This Loomism will help you decorate your home with premium paintings you probably thought only the wealthy could afford. A picture by a well-known artist in good condition usually sports a hefty price tag. To compensate, look for less-than-perfect artwork. Just as there are "fixer-uppers" for antique furniture, there are paintings that need a little work. The next time you go antiquing, look in shops, galleries, or malls for paintings with problems. Bruised artwork is sold at cut-rate prices because upscale collectors shy away from damaged goods.

When you find an appealing artist-signed painting offered at a reduced price because of dirt or a small tear, follow the "hang 'em high" rule. A powerful French monarch may have been the first to use this strategy to hide flaws in his paintings.

This still life, possibly by Severin Roesen (German/ American 1810-1871), was less costly because of damage.

(Photo courtesy of Skinner's Auction Company)

In the late 1600s, when King Louis XIV of France constructed his chateau near Paris, building costs probably left him short of funds needed to maintain his royal art collection. So the Sun King, an art collector extraordinaire, wisely ordered many pictures to be placed high on the tall walls of Versailles, making close scrutiny virtually impossible. I don't know if this practice actually started with Louis XIV, but the story illustrates how flawed paintings can be displayed so they look truly regal. Even though your walls are probably lower than those in Versailles, you can use this Loomism to conceal problems.

Place a blemished signed picture over a tall cabinet, near a ceiling, or over a stairway to prevent a close inspection. It's amazing how a few feet of distance can erase imperfections.

Try a few simple repair techniques to camouflage boo-boos such as tears and bruised frames. Touch up a scarred frame with matching paint (available in small bottles of acrylic paint at crafts stores), and make a tear less visible by applying masking tape to the back side to bring the two flaps of the canvas closer together. I have used these methods more than once on my unroyal, yet beguiling-to-me collection. One of my favorite paintings depicts a beautiful nineteenth-century Dutch scene complete with windmill, canal, and medium-sized tear. Although my home is no Versailles, I followed the Sun King's tactic by placing it high on a wall in my foyer. Masking tape on the back helps keeps the gash discreet.

Consider having seriously damaged paintings professional-ly restored. Even after restoration costs, you'll probably have paid only half the price of a similar picture in near-perfect condition.

YOUR ANTIQUES CEILING FOR SIGNED, TATTERED PAINTINGS:

- Signed paintings, framed: $100
- Signed paintings, unframed: $50

LOOMISM THREE
Display 'em High

Americans seem to have a strong aversion to cracks and chips in antique china. European collectors, on the other hand, don't mind a blemished piece nearly as much. While visiting

· ·

*Display a damaged piece with
its bad side to the back of high shelf
and no one will be the wiser.*

· ·

Provence, I was strolling through a fantastic outdoor antiques market, which in French is called *brocante*. At this brocante near Avignon, I spotted a cache of dazzling ceramics. Many of the pieces had chips, stains, or cracks and were being offered, of course, at bargain prices. A less than pristine pitcher charmed me. Its seller told me (as only the French so enchantingly can), "Monsieur, display it with its bad side to the back of a high shelf, and no one will be the wiser." I followed her guidance and paid $25, rather $100 for an unmarred piece, saving $75. Only the dealer, my bookcase, and I know it's not unblemished. Don't miss out on a beautiful ceramic piece at a terrific price just because it doesn't look so-called "museum perfect."

That brings up another point concerning less-than-pristine china. The next time you're touring a museum, examine the ceramic displays. As you leave, you may find yourself saying, "If defects are good enough for this world-famous institution, then they're certainly okay for me." That was exactly our reaction after our visit to the incredible Oriental Ceramics Gallery at the Art Institute of Chicago.

I have one final piece of advice concerning damaged ceramics: they are for display only, and never for dining.

Your Antiques Ceiling for
Damaged Ceramics:

- Small ceramic pieces less than 6 inches high or 8 inches in diameter, such as plates, pitchers, and vases: $10 each
- Larger pieces such as vases, teapots, platters, and big bowls: $25 each

 LOOMISM FOUR
Buy "Unpedigreed" Paintings for Excellent Savings

The Sensual Approach to Learning provides multiple opportunities for sharpening antiquing skills. One way is by thumbing through auction catalogues to study the prices paintings fetch. Such self-tutoring can teach you, for example, why one painting sells for five times more than another, even though the two seem equally gorgeous. Your research will soon reveal that the difference in cost lies not in beauty, but in status.

Is this canvas portraying a Victorian room any less beautiful because it lacks a signature?

(Photo courtesy of Skinner's Auction Company)

Pictures by celebrated painters have instant status. Artists who have not yet achieved such acclaim are considered second tier until critics and the media tout them. But remember that lack of fame doesn't necessarily mean second-rate, just unpublicized. Fortunately, the temporary lack of status makes them far less costly. Does prestige make a painting any more wonderful? Only to the insecure. In the eye of the beholder, a "Smith" landscape can be just as exciting as a Van Gogh.

· ·

Lack of fame doesn't necessarily mean second-rate, just unpublicized. Fortunately, the temporary lack of status makes them far less costly.

· ·

I found a 1970s watercolor that reminded me of southern France. As a tight-fisted collector, I was thrilled with the final negotiated price of $20 (using one of the antiques jocks methods, of course). The next day the appraiser in me took over, and I researched the signature but discovered nothing about

the painter. That's just fine. In my heart my captivating water-color by an uncelebrated painter is just as precious as a mas-terpiece by a renowned artist. No doubt Monsieur Renoir would enthusiastically concur.

Buying a painting that belonged to the great Greta Garbo will cost its owner many pret-ty pennies.

(Photo courtesy of Skinner's Auction Company)

Your Antiques Ceiling for paintings by second-tier artists:

- Framed: $150
- Unframed: $75

LOOMISM FIVE

Anonymous Art Is Especially Affordable

What type of painting can have an even kinder price than a damaged picture or a picture by a second-string artist? An anonymous painting is usually much less costly than a work with a signature, even a signed one by an uncelebrated painter. To me, an unsigned painting is like a bouquet of col-

This work by Frank Benson, who is known for depicting birds, gives testimony to the affordability of prints. It was given a pre-auction estimate of $250 to $350 complete with frame!

(Photo courtesy of Skinner's Auction Company)

orful wild flowers. Is a bunch of freshly picked Black-eyed Susans any less radiant than a bouquet of costly long-stemmed roses? Just as few seem to appreciate the beauty of wild flowers in a vase, it's the same with unsigned pictures. Bargains galore can be found in anonymous paintings.

Antiquers use the expression, "It yelled at me," to explain an antique's allure. An antique once yelled at me in one of my favorite shops—Lesterhouse Antiques in Mattawan, Michigan. Something wonderful caught my eye as Debbie and I entered. An ornate frame held a stunning oil landscape of trees and a river so realistically captured on canvas that it almost looked like a photo. The shop's owner, Bill, told me it was a Hudson River Valley scene painted around 1850 to 1875. Such scenes rendered by famous or even second-tier artists highlighting the Hudson River in upstate New York can go for thousands. For this delightful slice of Americana, the dealer offered his best price of $325, which I enthusiastically accepted. Because it lacked the signature of a "Mary Cassatt" or even a "Jane Doe," it was an incredible buy. You can find very affordable anonymous artworks in other medias, including watercolor, sculpture, textile, and metal work, just to name a few.

YOUR ANTIQUES CEILING FOR ANONYMOUS ART:

- Framed: $75
- Unframed: $35

 LOOMISM SIX
Think Unframed Prints

Paintings seem to go hand-in-hand with prints, one of the best deals in antiques you'll ever find. Parisian antiques have the reputation of being extremely expensive, but this is certainly not the case with old prints. If you want to get the most for your antiques dollar, or in this case, your antiques euros, think unframed prints. Not far from the Louvre Museum and its masterpiece, the "Mona Lisa," is the Left Bank, where many shops sell antique prints.

. . . .

Prints are one of the best deals in antiques you'll ever find. If you want to get the most for your money, think prints.

. . . .

Dianne, Pete, and I bought small bird prints for about $1.90 each there and didn't even try to negotiate because they were under $10. (They probably would have cost even less in smaller French towns, but we were only visiting Paris.) The colorful unframed prints came from 1880s French magazines. Back home, I bought ready-made frames and took them to my framer for custom-made mats. I picked overscaled mats and frames because that's how the French present their pictures.

These 1930s and 1940s prints may often be purchased for under $10.

(Author's collection)

Whether you're antiquing in Paris, France, or Paris, Kentucky, keep unframed prints on your shopping lists because they're such steals.

YOUR ANTIQUES CEILING FOR PRINTS:

- Framed, any size: $50
- Unframed, any size: $20

LOOMISM SEVEN
Avoid Hometown Antiques

My visits to the charming and historic cities of Savannah, Georgia, and Charleston, South Carolina, gave me more shopping expertise. Since I had recently discovered the great value of unframed antique prints, it seemed prudent to buy a few depicting these two antique havens of the South. While shopping for scenes of Savannah, I learned another antiquing trick. Although it seems backwards, it made great financial sense. You see, in Savannah I found 1880s prints depicting Charleston. Even though the shop catered to tourists, the prints were only $5 each. They would have cost far more if I had found them on swanky King Street in their hometown of Charleston.

Avoid buying antiques in their hometown or state of origin if you can resist the temptation. Chances are that everyone appreciates them more in their birthplace, which makes finding bargains almost impossible. So don't look for fine 1900 ceramic vases by Grueby Art Pottery in

Budget antiquers should avoid buying Newcomb Art Pottery in New Orleans, Louisiana, where it was created.

(Photo courtesy of Skinner's Auction Company)

Your chances for buys are much better if you avoid buying Grueby pottery in Boston, Massachusetts, its hometown.

(Photo courtesy of Skinner's Auction Company)

Boston. In Ohio, never pick molded 1930s Heisey Glass or colorful floral vases or bookends manufactured by Weller Pottery if you expect a deal. When antiquing in New Orleans, suppress your hankering for world-class ceramics dating from the early 1900s by Newcomb Art Pottery, and during a California visit, pass on Franciscan pottery so famous for the "Desert Rose" china pattern. Instead, shop for these antiques everywhere except in their hometown or state of origin.

YOUR ANTIQUES CEILING FOR
HOMETOWN ANTIQUES: $0

• At this stage of your antiques game, skip hometown antiques.

 LOOMISM EIGHT
Provenance Equals Priceyness

Perhaps a real estate agent coined the saying, "George Washington slept here." If so, the agent was probably attempting to increase the marketability of an old house by giving it a fictional historic past. In modern times, a genuine historic past, or provenance, is sometimes emphasized to raise the price of an antique. As a prospective buyer flirts with an antique, the seller sweetens its appeal by chronicling the history of its ownership. In Chicago, you might hear that it came from the estate of Marshall Field, the famous department store magnate. In Baltimore, a dealer might explain that an

item belonged to relatives of legendary silversmiths, the Kirk family. Each area of the country has charismatic names that heighten the desirability and value of an antique. It is fascinating to observe how much a pedigreed provenance can increase the value of an antique. The more famous the former owner, the more expensive the object becomes.

As you may recall in the auction chapter, I said that both the Greta Garbo and Jackie Kennedy estate auctions had broken all price records. The Garbo sale illustrates the influence of provenance. When Sotheby's in New York City auctioned her painting *A Woman in White, Seated,* by French artist Albert Andre (1869-1954), it sold for about $170,000. That

Your antiques coach learned a long time ago to avoid buying Rookwood in Cincinnati, its birthplace.

(Photo courtesy of Middletown Journal)

. . . .

It is fascinating to observe how much a pedigreed provenance can increase the value of an antique. The more famous the former owner, the more expensive the object becomes.

. . . .

was four times more than any other work of his has ever fetched at auction. Doesn't it seem logical that after the Garbo sale, all his paintings would achieve equally high prices? But

Originally part of President Polk's service in the late 1840s, this French plate has an appealing provenance; but it is smarter to pass on such illustrious pieces.

(Photo courtesy of Skinner's Auction Company)

they didn't; none had the appeal of a Garbo provenance. A few years later, Sotheby's auctioned one of his works for $23,000. The Garbo painting went for so much because of show biz and ego. With such a provenance, the new owner, if he or she so chooses, could gloat, "This painting belonged to Garbo." It's a mighty costly boast and one, I might add, that would disappoint Monsieur Renoir.

Your Antiques Ceiling for antiques
with a provenance: $0

•   Buy antiques that belonged to Jane or John Doe.

To stretch your purchasing power, avoid antiques with a stellar provenance.

(Photo courtesy of Skinner's Auction Company)

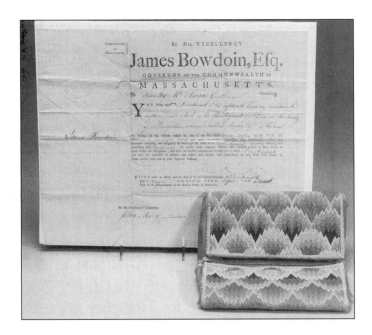

Bargain collectors should avoid antiques described with the following words: "with a museum label." Garth's supplied this provenance in its catalogues.

(Photo courtesy of Garth's Auctions, Inc.)

LOOMISM NINE
Leave Museum Quality to the Jet Set

When museums reduce their collections, they call the process de-accessioning. Auction houses are constantly competing for the opportunity to sell de-accessioned pieces, which lets them proudly tout museum provenance in their catalogues. When a sale's description proudly states, "From the Museum of XYZ" in its advertisement, this translates as, "Museum quality and it's going to cost mucho coin." Like the Garbo painting, the new owner may want to crow, "This table came from the Museum of XYZ."

You'll rarely find any buys among antiques with museum provenance. Visit places where such grand merchandise is being offered, take a good gander, and maybe touch them ever so gently so you get familiar with top-notch pieces. Then one day you may recognize a comparable antique with a far more affordable price because it lacks museum pedigree.

YOUR ANTIQUES CEILING FOR
MUSEUM QUALITY: $0

- Avoid museum quality and stick with non-institutional pieces.

LOOMISM TEN

Pass On Pairs

Pairs of antiques such as these German vases from the 1800s usually cost more than two bought separately.

(Photo courtesy of Skinner's Auction Company)

Pairs of antiques are always more expensive than two similar single versions. Whether you're looking at a pair of authentic 1825 prints, a pair of 1930s Roseville vases, or a pair of 1960s chairs, duos cost more. A pair of china vases from the 1880s made by the Haviland firm in Limoges, France, retails for $250. They're each worth about 25 percent more as part of a set than they are individually. So a single vase would retail for about $100. Choose singles and then mate them. By buying

Buy two similar-looking singles and mate them to save 20 percent or more.

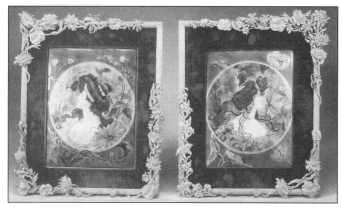

These two 1900 beauties cost more because they are a duo.

(Photo courtesy of Skinner's Auction Company)

two different but similar vases for $200, you'll save about 20 percent (or sometimes even more.) If one is chipped—wonderful! The savings, as you know, can even be even greater. Just remember what the French dealer at the brocante said about finding a high spot to display them.

Your Antiques Ceiling for pairs: $0

- Think singles and focus on marriages.

Not many collectors could afford this charismatic pair of portraits of Millie and Lottie Darling painted around 1840 by American artist extraordinaire William Matthew Prior. Pre-auction estimates were $30,000 to $50,000.

(Photo courtesy of Skinner's Auction Company)

LOOMISM ELEVEN
Avoid Sets

Just as I recommend avoiding pairs of most antiques, I urge you to do the same with sets of furniture pieces. This is especially shrewd advice for bedroom and dining room antiques.

. . . .

Although chairs were made in sets
for centuries, other household furniture
rarely came that way.

. . . .

General and Mrs. Washington did not have a matching piece in their bedroom at Mount Vernon.

(Photo courtesy of Mt. Vernon Ladies' Society)

Although chairs were made in sets for centuries, other household furniture rarely came that way. Homes in the 1700s were decorated with unmatched but similarly shaped and sized furnishings. There's not a matching bedroom or dining suite to be found at Mount Vernon. The canopy bed, chest of drawers, and washstand in George and Martha's bedroom all worked beautifully together because they had similar styles and proportions.

Around the 1840s, the French began creating matching pieces of furniture, usually for dining rooms or bedrooms,

called "suites" in English. According to the *Larousse French-English Dictionary*, the more correct French word for matched sets is "ensemble." In French, "suite" literally means "a continuation of one after another." Words, particularly those involving antiques, often get twisted when they're adopted from another language. Somehow "suite," which is the origin of our English word "suit," pertaining to furniture, has stuck to this day.

To get more for your money, avoid buying bedroom suites.

(Photo courtesy of Middletown Journal)

> *Especially avoid purchasing sets of bedroom and dining room furniture. Mate odd pieces together in antiques marriages.*

As always, the British and the Americans followed the lead of French trendsetters. Suddenly, Victorian homes featured sets/suites/suits for virtually every room of the house, which was considered the height of fashion in the late 1800s.

My advice is to avoid purchasing sets. Think of the buying power of "oneness." Purchase pieces individually. Choose a table for your dining room that blends nicely with a china closet, or select a vanity that complements the bed in your bedroom. By purchasing your antiques piecemeal, you can buy two for the price of one. Odd pieces mated into antiques marriages (or what I like to call "semi-suites") can often save you more than 50 percent. So have romance on your mind when looking for furniture and think antiques weddings.

YOUR ANTIQUES CEILING FOR SETS/SUITES/SUITS: $0

- Buy single pieces with "semi-sets/suites/suits" in mind.
- See the Antiques Ceiling under Loomism One for prices of individual pieces.

An "assembled" set of chairs designates that they are not original to each other, therefore reducing their value.

(Photo courtesy of Skinner's Auction Company)

LOOMISM TWELVE
Unmatched Chairs: Single Is Best

Seating was crafted into matching groups long before Columbus first sailed for the New World. Chairs were usually made in groups of four, six, eight, or even twelve. Generally, as the number of antique chairs in a suite increases, the price per chair also increases.

Of any piece of furniture you can buy, single side chairs are absolutely the best value. That's why I love them. Look for quality unmated side chairs about the same height and proportion and with similarly shaped legs. Be sure to find them either in the same wood or similar shade (such as medium walnut with dark oak) and purchase them singly. Pass on armchairs because they cost proportionately more. Although it may take more time to find the number you want, focus on the fun you'll have looking for just the right and oh-so-affordable chairs. (Never forget to give any prospective candidates the posterior test before you buy.) When you have the quantity you need, cover the seats with your favorite fabric. Matching upholstery magically unites odd chairs into what

Matching suites of chairs always cost more.

(Photo courtesy of Skinner's Auction Company)

. . . .

Although it may take time to find the number of chairs you want, think of the fun you'll have looking for them.

. . . .

appears to be a suite. By acquiring your chairs one at a time, you'll fork out 75 percent less than the price of a genuine suite.

A few years ago, I found a 1790 English chair with a wheel-shaped back and square-tapered legs for a mere $75. If it were part of a genuine set of six, the whole suite could easily have cost $4,500. By buying six unmated chairs at $75 to $100 each,

. . . .

When you have the quantity of chairs
you need, upholster them to make
them look like a suite.

. . . .

you'll pay $450 to $600 for a "married" suite rather than $4,500, or about ten times as much, for an original set. That English chair blends stylishly with my others, and guests have rarely noticed it's not part of a typical suite. Call these custom-married chairs "semi-suites," just as we do with unmated bedroom or dining pieces.

YOUR ANTIQUES CEILING FOR UNMATCHED
CHAIRS: $100 EACH

 LOOMISM THIRTEEN
Give Monogrammed Flatware
Your Stamp of Approval

The monograms on this early 1900s sterling silver traveling set lowered its pre-auction estimate to $400 to $600.

(Photo courtesy of Skinner's Auction Company)

Cutlery is another antique that many people like to collect. When buying old silver, choose monogrammed flatware, which costs less than non-initialed utensils. I recently paid $19 for a monogrammed dinner fork, while the unmarked one

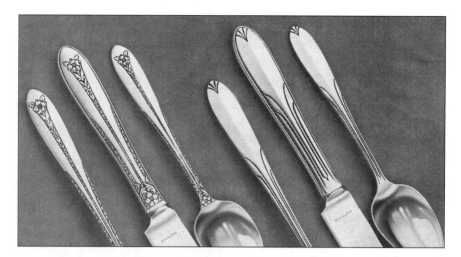

was almost double. The seller told me I was the only person she ever met who wanted monogrammed silver because, according to her, "Everyone wants plain pieces." My reply: "I like the lower prices of the engraved pieces."

In these days of stainless steel and throwaway plastic cutlery, fine silver is a wonderful keepsake recalling a more gracious past. So be prepared for compliments when you lay out your silver service. When your guests spot those initials, they'll ask if your flatware is a family heirloom. Just smile and say, "Why yes, they are family pieces." Be proud of your homeruns as an antiquer, and set the record straight by truthfully adding, "Of course, other people's family pieces."

Monograms can also increase your purchasing power with other silver and silver-plated pieces, as well as various linens, including napkins and tablecloths.

Sterling silver flatware from the 1930s and 1940s can have the sweetest prices.

(Author's collection)

Your Antiques Ceiling for monogrammed sterling silver flatware:

- Dinner knives, dinner forks, salad forks, butter knives: $18 each
- Serving pieces such as tablespoons, etc: $40 each
- See Chapter 17, Loomism Three, for your antiques ceiling for linens.

LOOMISM FOURTEEN
Worn Carpets Give Deals You Won't Want to Sweep Under the Rug

Carpets from the Near East or the Orient have been crafted for centuries and look fantastic with anything in your home,

Is this antique Oriental rug damaged? It may or may not be.
It's amazing how defects seem to disappear once you get home.

(Photo courtesy of Garth's Auctions, Inc.)

whether under a 1700s spindleback Windsor chair or beneath a modern leather sofa. Top-dollar carpets are made of wool, show no fading or tears, and are unsullied by pets.

As rugs become worn and faded, they acquire a weathered look akin to the patina of antique furniture. However, one of the worst nightmares for a seller occurs when a pet has tainted a beautiful piece. That flaw can slash the price by 50 percent or more, which is a great boon for us. After a thorough cleaning, the carpet's various colors can camouflage the damage. A perk of buying blemished rugs is that the worn look will give your home some heirloom status, and guests will assume it was your grandmother's.

Your Antiques Ceiling for worn or stained Persian or Oriental rugs:

- 6 feet x 9 feet: $300
- 9 feet x 12 feet: $500

LOOMISM FIFTEEN
Get a Handle on Replaced Handles

Not all blemishes on antiques are as serious as torn carpets or broken chair legs. Sometimes a defect is so minor that it's detectable only to an expert. Do you remember how the

. . . .

Not all blemishes are serious. Sometimes they are so minor that they are only detectable to an expert.

. . . .

replaced pulls made my highboy even more affordable? Honest dealers like the Browns always point out the less noticeable imperfections such as non-original handles, which will reduce the price about 25 percent. The replaced pulls/handles should be good quality and similar to the originals. It would be an antiques faux pas to have ornate Victorian-era handles on a plain 1780s chest of drawers.

YOUR ANTIQUES CEILING FOR A PIECE OF FURNITURE WITH REPLACED HANDLES:

- 75 percent of the price of a piece with original handles (To get a handle on prices of perfect examples, follow the tips in Chapter 9 for comparison shopping.)

LOOMISM SIXTEEN
Antiques Unions Are a Match Made in Heaven

This tip is one more case of how really clever our ancestors were and gives us another way to get first-class antiques for much less. Quality antique furniture, such as cabinets, highboys, and corner cupboards, were usually crafted in two pieces, which eased the task of moving them. For various reasons through the years, bases and tops were sometimes divorced from their significant other. Purists who are willing to pay top dollar insist that both sections must be original to each other.

. . . .

Antiques marriages make some fabulous pieces from the 1700s affordable even to budget-conscious collectors.

. . . .

Straightforward dealers and auctioneers always identify antiques marriages. When you look at the front of a cupboard, the top and bottom may appear original to each other, but the honest professional discloses that the back wooden panels don't match. The upper boards may be a different size, wood, or color from the lower ones, which is a dead giveaway about a merger. This imperfection is an invitation to budget antiquers! You probably recall that Darlene Brown stated that my highboy was a merger. Even to this day, I say it was a match made in antiques heaven.

If you're buying a married piece, make sure top and bottom are well mated. They should have the same size, style, and wood. You don't want a top section too small for the base or crafted from a different timber. If your first impression didn't scream, "Put together," that's a good sign.

Properly married pieces keep costs down. What some consider a shortcoming opens the collecting door to fabulous pieces from the 1700s that, if completely genuine, only tycoons or museums could afford. Also remember that neither quality nor good looks has been sacrificed and only the wall knows your secret.

YOUR ANTIQUES CEILING FOR MARRIED PIECES: 50 PERCENT OF AN ALL-ORIGINAL PIECE (WITH TOP SECTION ORIGINAL TO BOTTOM SECTION).

- Check out perfect examples by following the tips in Chapter 9 for comparison shopping to get a realistic idea for prices.

LOOMISM SEVENTEEN
Geography Affects Success

Choosing the most advantageous area to shop can make you an Olympic champion in the sport of antiquing. That real estate principle "location, location, location" certainly applies to uncovering the areas with the friendliest prices.

. . . .

That real estate principle "location, location, location" certainly applies to uncovering the areas with the friendliest prices.

. . . .

Avoid heavy-duty shopping in big cities. It has been my wearisome experience that antiques cost proportionately more in New York, Chicago, New Orleans, Atlanta, Boston, and San Francisco. The benefit of these metropolitan areas, however, is that although they aren't usually favorable for antiquing on a shoestring, they always have superb shops, auction houses, and, of course, museums so conducive to tutoring sessions.

Forgive me, those of you who live on the East Coast or West Coast of the United States, but the "Mid Coast" (my pet name for the Midwest) offers the best deals. Antiques are more affordable west of the Hudson River and east of the Rocky

. . . .

Antiques are more affordable west of the
Hudson River and east of the Rocky Mountains
(and yes, even in the bigger cities).

. . . .

Mountains (and yes, even in the bigger cities). So many times I have spotted dealers buying merchandise in shops, malls, and auctions all located within this vast heartland of antiques. Although the dealers try to be ever so discreet so they don't give away trade secrets, I can spot them every time. Follow their example by focusing on the "Mid Coast."

When traveling in high tourists areas, as I cautioned you earlier, only window shop in antiques shops catering to travelers. Although down-to-earth prices may be rare, apply the Sensual Approach to Learning as you play tourist and antiquer-in-training.

Canada and Mexico also have wonderful and affordable antiques. South of the border, try the smaller towns away from Mexico City; in Canada explore the western provinces like Alberta and Manitoba.

When on holiday in Europe, visit museums in London, Paris, Rome, and other historic places. Then do your serious antiquing in small towns located in the vicinity of these glorious cities. When in France, be sure to visit the brocantes I mentioned previously. Check with local tourist centers wherever you go for locations and schedules of similar outdoor

markets. The prices can be so low compared to what you would pay in large metropolitan centers.

ANOTHER PLUG FOR DEFECTS/OPPORTUNITIES

It's important to reiterate that chips and dents on your antiques—earned through years of use and love by their own- ers—offer double bonuses to bargain antiquers. Their patina makes them look old like antiques should, yet that delightful quality renders them less costly than pristine versions. So now is the right moment to mention another perk about less than picture-perfect antiques. Have you ever been in a house where every antique looks faultless? Did you feel cozy, or were you afraid to even sit on a chair? Remember, antiques are old and they're supposed to have flaws. That's what makes them so charming. Let those who prefer perfect antiques pay big bucks. We'll use our liberal outlook about condition (but not quality) to our advantage.

Some collectors may brand the monograms on these sterling silver pitchers a blemish, but we don't.

(Photo courtesy of Skinner's Auction Company)

16

Antique Gifts Equal More Buys

BEING AN ANTIQUES GOOD SAMARITAN MAKES SENSE AND SAVE CENTS

A display of antique gifts at the Middletown Antiques Mall.

(Photo courtesy of Middletown Journal)

Please don't fall off your antique chair as you read this, but I have no more sermons about the affordability of antiques. I do, however, have a final secret to divulge. This brainstorm, which hit me a few Christmases ago, has not only brought me much joy, but has also stretched my budget. I'm confident it

can do the same for you. It's a simple but joyful truth: it's better to give antiques than brand-new presents as gifts.

I became an Antiques Good Samaritan during a shopping excursion one Saturday in December. My antiquing comrades and I met at a shopping center to carpool. When I arrived at the mall (the non-antiques variety), I hunted and hunted for a parking place. After ten minutes and much frustration, I

· ·

It's a simple but joyful truth:
it's better to give antiques than
brand-new presents as gifts.

· ·

finally landed one of the very few empty spots. After leaving that place of Christmas Pandemonium, we spent a delightful, tranquil, crowd-free afternoon at several antiques malls. That's what finally lit my antiques light bulb. "Bingo! From now on I'm giving antiques for Christmas, Hanukkah, birthdays, weddings, and you name-it occasions," I said as I spotted some good buys, including a framed 1930s charcoal drawing of a dog priced at $15. (I must confess that in this case I was an Antiques Good Samaritan to myself.)

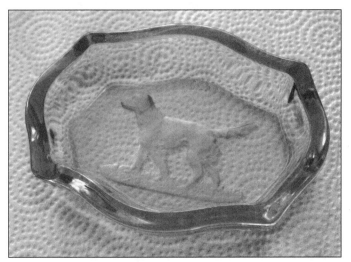

This semi-antique/collectible was made by the famous Heisey Glass of Ohio and appeals to canine lovers.

(Photo courtesy of Middletown Journal)

Wouldn't this papier-mâché figure used for advertising Victrolas in the early 1900s appeal to a dog lover or advertising collector?

(Photo courtesy of Skinner's Auction Company)

As you know, antiques come with great perks such as affordability and getting more for your hard-earned cash. This chapter demonstrates that when you give antiques as gifts, you get these perks and more.

Imagine your panache when you hand someone a present and say, "I hope you like this. It's antique." The saying, "It's better to give than to receive" is absolutely correct. My embellished version is, "It's better to give antiques rather than new gifts." Envision how pleasurable it will be every time you see your gift in the recipient's home. So, as you can see, this gift strategy really makes sense and saves cents, too, while adding a whole new dimension to the benefits that antiques bring.

If you aren't certain what to share with someone, choose an item related to what the person enjoys. For pet lovers, a small figurine of a dog or cat should be a hit. Whether you choose an upscale English china pooch by Royal Doulton or a less costly yet equally charming version from Japan, it will be appreciated. One year, I gave my sister, as part of her gifts, a little beauty that only set me back $2. But to my sister, it was worth a million sentimentally because she is just as nutty about dogs as most of us are.

A SENSUAL-APPROACH CLASS

One of my favorite classes at the University of Cincinnati was a hands-on application of the principles of this book. Our last session took the Sensual Approach to Learning and Safe Antiquing to the ultimate as my students spent the day antiquing at huge malls in Springfield, Ohio.

To describe these places as mammoth is truly an understatement because they have a total of over six hundred dealers in the malls. Arriving at these emporiums gives the antiquer such a thrill. It's easy to understand the excitement shoppers felt in the old days when they arrived at Herald Square in Manhattan. Side by side were Macy's and Gimbel's—two

. . . .

If you aren't certain what to share with someone, choose an item related to what the person enjoys. For pet lovers, a small figurine of a dog or cat should be a hit.

. . . .

gigantic department stores ready to seduce shoppers. That's the same feeling I got but stronger because Springfield offers three huge venues. My group started at 10 a.m. on a Saturday morning, ate a quick lunch at one of the malls, then continued antiquing/learning.

As we were eating, Sandy, one of my students, told us she was looking for water goblets to go with her grandmother's French china. She asked me if she would have to pay $30 to $40 per glass. "Never!" I said. "I want you to pay about $8 to $10 each." After lunch, I told my group we were on a shopping mission for Sandy to find stemware that cost less than $10 each.

Since this was a class, naturally I had given an assignment besides shopping for Sandy. Students had to look for items in prices ranging from under $10 to the extremely high amount of $100. These prices were before negotiation, which, as you understand, can result in substantial reductions.

When we stopped at 4 p.m., my enthusiastic students/antiquers and I compiled the following list, which illustrates how antiques make unique yet affordable gifts.

The Shopping List

Under $10

- One water goblet, circa 1930s $1.50
  The class really enjoyed searching for Sandy's water goblets. Thanks to their efforts, she had several choices. She chose a set of eight. A chip on the base of one made it unbelievably low-priced. It matched the seven others, for which Sandy paid $8.50 each. As she wisely said, "No one will even notice it, and it isn't unsanitary or anything." Incidentally, an emory file soon smoothed over that chip. Well done, Sandy!
- Small china doll from Japan, circa 1950s $2.
- French china plate, 8-inch diameter, circa 1900 $3.
- Sandy's other matching seven water goblets, circa 1930s, in good condition, each $8.50
- Solid wood tennis racket with brace, circa 1950s $9.50

$10 TO $50

- Pressed-tin ceiling panel, framed in
  barn wood siding, circa 1910 $10.
- Hobnailed glass vase, 6 inches high,
  circa 1940s $25.
- Wedgwood china demitasse cup and saucer,
  circa 1920s $28.
- Pair of iron claw feet from a claw-foot
  bathtub, circa 1910 $35.
- Carved wooden Chinese panel, circa 1910 $35.

$50 TO $100

- Child's rocking chair, circa 1940s $50.
- Adult walnut sewing rocking chair,
  circa 1890 $65.
- Cut glass bowl, circa 1900 $69.
- Victorian china statue of a lady, circa 1880 $85.
- Console TV set, circa 1950s (Retro!) $95.

Old decoys are a natural gift for a man who thinks he has everything.

(Photo courtesy of Skinner's Auction Company)

GO GENERIC

Don't you agree this is quite an impressive list? It certainly demonstrates that antiques make inexpensive, thoughtful, and unique gifts. If you are still debating what to give, go generic. Avoid a heavy-duty antique, such as a certain type of china vase or a very ornate chair. Pick something instead that is eclectic and belongs to no particular style or area of antiques.

Old books make wonderful and inexpensive presents.

(Photo courtesy of Skinner's Auction Company)

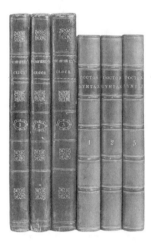

For example, the framed pressed-tin ceiling panel (removed from an old building and in the $10 section) would really make an excellent gift for a high school or college graduate. This slice of American history is not the least bit fussy and has the kind of price that Gimbel's bargain basement was known for.

RECYCLING/DE-CLUTTERING/GIFTS

Here's another advantage to giving antiques as gifts. Earlier, you learned how one of the oldest forms of recycling is antiquing. Later we looked at how to de-clutter by selling no-longer-needed items. Here is a favorite method that I have used on many occasions.

Old magazines such as *Life* make great gifts.

(Photo courtesy of Middletown Journal)

Ever since becoming an uncle, I have tried to get Ryan and "Miss" Mackenzie hooked on antiques. Well, Ryan is a true

antiques success story. These days, as I told you earlier, he is quite interested in Retro semi-antiques/collectibles. My efforts with his sister, on the other hand, were less than stellar—until her wedding, that is.

When "Miss" Mackenzie married Kris, I followed the example of my grandmother, who often gave me cherished family mementos as Christmas or birthday presents. You may recall that she had given me a ruby glass souvenir from the 1893 World's Fair.

A wonderful idea for new parents and baby: a riding or gliding horse.

(Photo courtesy of Skinner's Auction Company)

- -

Gifting is a form of de-accessioning by recycling no-longer-needed treasures like family pieces or collected items.

- -

When special times approach, all you need to do is follow my smart Gram's lead by scrutinizing your home. Perhaps your home is like mine and is bordering on spilling over.

HARRY S. TRUMAN
INDEPENDENCE, MISSOURI

RET'D SEP 4 1958

August 30 , 1958

Dear Mike:

I am enclosing the cards you sent to me for signature
on June 30th. Unfortunately, they were at the bottom
of the great pile of mail that accumulated here while I
was gone.

Miss Anna Elgin's letter is being returned too so you
can have it where it will do the most good.

I apologize for the delay, but circumstances made it
unavoidable.

Sincerely yours,

Harry Truman

*When things like this happen I'm not
sure I'm as efficient
as I was in times past*

Hon. A. S. Mike Monroney
United States Senate
Washington, D. C.

Encs.

Autographs are a fun and exciting gifting adventure. Mr. Truman's is probably a little too rich
for most collectors, but plenty of affordable "John Hancocks" are out there.

(Photo courtesy of Skinner's Auction Company)

Gifting is a form of de-accessioning by recycling no-longer-needed treasures like family pieces or collected items.

As I keep trying to remind you (and especially myself), I make it a practice to remove a current antique when I get a

. . . .

Make it a practice to remove a current antique when you buy a new one. Otherwise, you may find your house becoming cluttered.

. . . .

new one. Otherwise, the paths in my home would become even narrower. Last year I bought an English cupboard, so I needed to recycle a charming 1940s mahogany corner china closet. I was going to consign it to a favorite mall, but in the middle of the night, my antiques light bulb lit up: it would make a grand wedding present for my niece and her fiancé.

While giving the china closet that magical tender loving care I told you about earlier, I found the manufacturer's label. The Grand Rapids Chair Company of Grand Rapids, Michigan, had made it. The groom is from that former furniture-manufacturing city, so I thought this information would put the icing on their antiques wedding cake. As usual, the appraiser in me took over; I found its mark in my copy of *Grand Rapids Furniture* by Christian G. Carron, verifying its 1940s origin. I made a photocopy of Mr. Carron's research, which I attached to the back of the piece.

LOOMISM

We all have impulsive moments for buying things. By choosing antiques as presents, you're filling your hunger for shopping. This good deed saves you from spending unnecessary money and from cluttering your home. Best of all, when gift time arrives, you're ready!

A day before the wedding, my sister, Debbie; my brother-in-law, Ron; and I secretly delivered the cabinet to a special corner in their dining room. The cabinet looked spectacular in their new condo, but honestly, Uncle Frank was somewhat apprehensive. You see, the newlywed's home had no antiques except candlesticks given to her by you-know-whom. However, their new cherry furniture encouraged me because it was approximately the same color as the mahogany china closet. Remember those near twins, mahogany and cherry that I told you about in Chapter 6?

At home, we awaited the bride and groom's verdict. Would Uncle Frank end up a successful Antiques Good Samaritan or not? All three of us sighed with relief when "Miss" Mackenzie declared the china closet "perfect." A week later Debbie remarked that a parcel from two other Antiques Good Samaritans had arrived. Dianne and Pete had sent an antique French bowl that has become a standout in their cabinet. The newlywed's approval of both antiques reinforces my mission of making them antiquers. And no doubt someday their grandchildren will treasure these future heirlooms.

. . . .

Do consider making gifts of no-longer-needed gems, whether furniture, china, pictures, or anything else. This antiques strategy makes great sense because you can accomplish five tasks in one.

. . . .

Do consider making gifts of no-longer-needed gems, whether furniture, china, pictures, or anything else. This antiques strategy makes great sense because you can accomplish five tasks in one:

1. Become an Antiques Good Samaritan to share the joy and wonder of antiques.
2. Spruce up your home by getting rid of excess stuff.
3. Save money by giving your recyclables as gifts, which, as you now know so well, also helps save the environment by keeping dump heaps smaller.
4. Save precious time needed for shopping.
5. Virtually eliminate the chance that someone will give the same gift, because antiques are one of a kind.

The Whole Antiques Enchilada

Here is a final charming idea I learned from Karen Plunkett-Powell. Whenever my "Woolworth's" friend gave an antique gift, she wrapped it in old-fashioned-looking wrapping paper or in old doilies. Using doilies is a wonderful idea, and not the least bit expensive. Not too long ago at an outdoors show, I saw a huge box of beauties for $2 each. Doilies just seem to pull the whole package together while making it totally unique. (More about doilies in Chapter 17).

LOOMISM

The odds of giving someone a duplicate gift are much lower because antiques are usually one of a kind.

Donations to Goodwill/Salvation Army

Here's one final and really special way to practice being an Antiques Good Samaritan and keep clutter under control. Give your overstocked items to Goodwill, the Salvation Army, or any of the other wonderful charitable marts. You'll be doing a good deed. Be sure to get a receipt for your donation, as it should be a very legitimate tax deduction.

Beating Price Increases

FIVE SEMI-ANTIQUE/COLLECTIBLES I PREDICT WILL SKYROCKET IN VALUE

The antiques and semi-antiques/ collectibles in this chapter won't break your bank.

(Photo courtesy of Antiques Magazine)

Your antiques coach keeps encouraging you to be keen on antiques for the pleasure they convey, and that's gospel. But I always try to be frank with you, so I want to bring up another matter that has yet to be addressed. If you're like me, a certain question creeps into your mind as you scan the prices of

We Want to Buy Old Cast Iron Mechanical Penny Banks

BOY ON TRAPEZE

Toy Forts with Cannons, Buildings, Animals, Comics, Human Figures, Grotesques, etc. Who do various tricks and stunts, when a penny is placed in Bank. Please communicate with us regarding any such mechanical banks (or very rare and unusual banks of other varieties) which you have or may know about, or be able to obtain. If you will write the full description and name of the bank (if it has any), together with a sketch and state the lowest acceptable price, it will facilitate matters; but in any event, write us and we will reply promptly. SHERWOOD'S OLD PENNY BANKS, 2316 Third Avenue, Spring Lake, New Jersey.

WHIRLING CLOWN ON GLOBE

antiques and semi-antiques/collectibles: Which will increase in value? And which ones will increase the fastest?

I have developed the following Loomisms that predict which semi-antiques/collectibles (all recently purchased at antiques malls or shows) will go through the antiques roof. I think you'll find that these specific guidelines are not only enlightening but will save you money.

LOOMISM ONE
Look for Stangl Pottery

Stangl Pottery made dinnerware and figurines in Trenton, New Jersey, from 1930 to 1978. If you're looking for bargains, pass on this firm's stunning bird statues. Instead, choose Stangl tableware with a thick country look and decorated in brown and orange designs similar to Pennsylvania German pottery made in the 1800s. When you turn over a piece, you can easily see that is marked "Stangl."

. . . .

For bargains, look for Stangl tableware.

. . . .

You earlier read that I maintain a constant clutter patrol at the Chateau de Loomis. Trying not to be an antiques hypocrite dictates no new collections for me. But if I were to start a new antiques adventure, it would be Stangl.

Example: Dinner plate with central tulip design, circa 1960s.

Price: $5 in an antiques mall.

No negotiation was needed under $10. It made a great gift.

YOUR ANTIQUES CEILING FOR STANGL:

- Dinner plate, salad plate, bread and butter plate, or teacup and saucer: $10
- Serving pieces, such vegetable bowls, teapots, and platters: $30

Vintage 1930s and 1940s stemware are great values, as my class learned during our day at the Springfield Antiques Mall.
(Author's collection)

LOOMISM TWO
Buy Pressed and Molded Glass

When antique glass is mentioned, we most likely think of 1930s Depression glass. Although that type still has very friendly prices, I want you to go back another hundred years to the 1830s to find even better deals. Remember our discussion about the relationship between Industrial Revolution and the definition of antique? That's when glass manufacturing was modernized by mass-production methods. Examples from that era are standout buys.

Look for thick clunky pieces, which are so unlike our thin, delicate modern glass. Avoid cake stands, however, as the prices of those late-1800s and early 1900s beauties have exploded. All the fanfare in decorating magazines has no doubt made them more popular than ever which, as we all know, increases their price tremendously.

Example: Clear compote, 6 inches in height and diameter, circa 1870s

Price: $3

. . . .

Look for thick clunky pieces of glass, which are
so unlike our thin, delicate modern glass.
Avoid cake stands, however, as the prices
of those late-1800s and early 1900s
beauties have exploded.

. . . .

Without even thinking, I used the pause technique, and it worked! The dealer came down from $5. Hey—he offered—so I broke the "No Negotiation for Under $5 Rule" that applies to flea markets and other "Woolworth's." (The compote turned out to be a terrific Christmas gift.)

YOUR ANTIQUES CEILING FOR PRESSED OR MOLD-ED GLASS: FOR ANY PIECE, INCLUDING COMPOTES, PITCHERS, ETC.: $30

LOOMISM THREE:
Stock Up on Linens

Linens—whether placemats, napkins, doilies, sheets, dresser scarves, or guest towels—can be even less expensive than glass. Pillowcases are the only exceptions because they have always been popular as wedding presents. Your choice of age, designs, and colors are as limitless as shapes and sizes. Elaborate doilies—looking as if they came from Aunt Pittypat's house in *Gone with the Wind*—are usually available, as are less ornate versions.

Example: A dresser scarf, circa 1920s

Price: $2

At less than $5, negotiation wasn't necessary.

It looks great in my living room on a cabinet.

YOUR ANTIQUES CEILING FOR LINENS:

- Dresser scarves: $5
- Guest towels: $5
- Napkins: $3
- Placemats: $4
- Tablecloths: $15

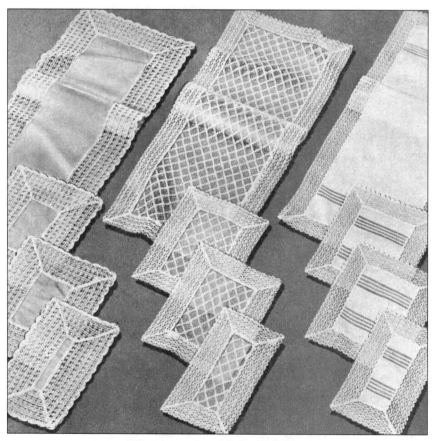

1940s linens are one of the best deals going.

(Author's collection)

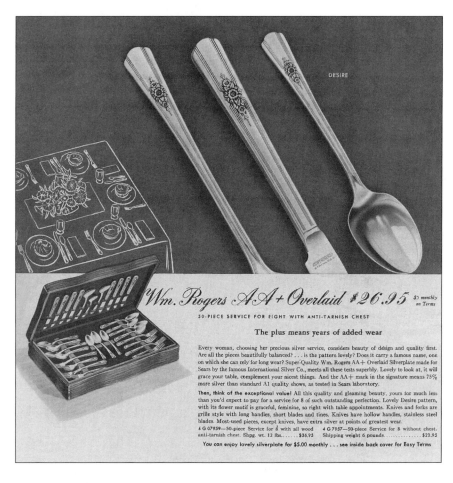

LOOMISM FOUR
Serve Up Silver-Plated Flatware

Silver-plated cutlery is another sensational antiques bargain. To get exceptional deals, "marry" single odd pieces with similar looking patterns into a set. The manufacturer's logo is usually stamped on the back, and some famous quality names include Reed & Barton, Rogers Brothers, Wallace, and Gorham. Knives, forks, spoons, and other pieces are available in many patterns, from ultraornate motifs dating from pre-World War I years to unadorned designs from the 1960s.

Julie's silver flatware resembles these pieces by famous manufacturer William Rogers.

(Author's collection)

Example: Dinner knives and forks, circa 1930s

Price: $1 each

Someday, current prices will seem as low as this 1937 quote of $18.50 for 1790-1820 silver-plated candlesticks!

(Photo courtesy of Antiques Magazine)

I gratefully owe this example to Julie, one of my students, who found these pieces at one of those malls I told you about in the Antiques Good Samaritan chapter. She wisely followed my advice not to negotiate for an item under $10 in a mall. It may be hard to believe, but the monogram matched her last name. Bravo, Julie!

YOUR ANTIQUES CEILING FOR MONOGRAMMED SILVER PLATE FLATWARE: ANY PIECE, $1 EACH

LOOMISM FIVE

Collect Postcards

What could be more affordable than silver-plated flatware, yet be headed for major price increases? Postcards! This antique is so affordable that at times even I can't believe it. Postcards were invented in Austria in 1869. Since then, they have been produced by the millions, which keep them affordable. These beautiful insights into of the past captured daily life long before any of us were born. Pick your favorite postcard sub-

Here's my fifty-five cent postcard showcasing a beautiful antique building.

(Author's collection)

ject, such as urban, pastoral, historical, or perhaps whimsical, and follow my earlier brainstorm about using custom-made mats with ready-made frames to get stylish artwork costing almost nothing.

Example: 1916 Postcard of New York City showing the Liberty Tower (thirty stories) located at Nassau and Liberty.

Price: 55 cents

The seller created his own variation of my "two-for" deal. His "five-for" deal featured five postcards for $2.55. Tight-fisted me, I took him up on his offer. I think my chipper "Hello" (as I told you earlier to practice) got us off to a good start.

- -

Purchase postcards and place them in custom-made mats with ready-made frames to get stylish artwork costing almost nothing.

- -

Even better, this postcard contained an unexpected historical bonus. On September 3, 1916, while on holiday in Manhattan, Ralph wrote the following note to John on the back of the postcard:

"Trying to find our way around in N.Y. City. Believe you have to lay on your back when you look at the top of some of these skyscrapers."

Ralph penned his observation before the Empire State Building and Chrysler Building were constructed, which proves that the impressiveness of a skyscraper is in the eye of the beholder.

YOUR ANTIQUES CEILING FOR POSTCARDS: $3

So, there are my Loomisms for the five antiques or semi-antiques/collectibles I think will increase in value the most. Right now they are downright unbelievably low cost, so stock up soon. Someday you may look back at today's prices and wish you had bought more of them. Only time will tell if I am right about these gems.

You're about to graduate from the Loomis School of Antiques, but before you do, I'd like to share one last story and Loomism in the final chapter. You will really relish this charming and true account about an antiquer and her "déjà vu" semi-antique/collectible. I just have to share this story with you because it could happen to you, too.

PART VIII

GRADUATION

18

A Déjà-Vu Antique

A Great Collector is Born

My most rewarding tale about the thrill of antiques concerns
the unexpected joy that a semi-antique/collectible brought to
a fellow antiquer. Linda Lee Jolly is an addicted collector; like
us, she craves an antiques fix from time to time. Her favorite
way to reduce stress from her hectic schedule as the director
of the Troy-Hayner Cultural Center in Troy, Ohio, is to visit a
favorite antiques mall.

. . . .

Linda Lee states that her budget doesn't
allow her to be "a great collector," but she
truly did become one that afternoon.

. . . .

One particular antiquing excursion proved to be especially
rewarding. Although she didn't stumble on a million-dollar
painting or a solid silver tea set for the price of a plated service, she experienced a once-in-a-lifetime event.

Linda Lee states that her budget doesn't allow her to be "a
great collector," but she truly did become one that afternoon.
In one of the mall's booths, a little girl's red plastic purse from
the 1950s caught her eye. She later described it as "very
small—the size a little girl of three or four might possess."

Then she remembered that when she was that age, she had had a similar bag that was part of her Sunday outfit for church.

When Linda Lee checked the long strap on the purse, she was truly startled to discover that the original owner had chewed on the strap, just as she had on hers. That coincidence motivated her to buy it. Shortly afterwards, she realized it was her purse. It was the same one that had been bought for her when she lived in Fort Thomas, Kentucky!

How did her purse turn up more than forty years later in an antiques mall about a hundred miles north of where she last used it? Linda Lee and her mother finally decided she must have left it at her Aunt Mildred's house after a family get-together. Her aunt probably placed it in a drawer for safekeeping until her niece's return visit. After her aunt's death, an estate auction was conducted, attracting dealers from near and far. In large household sales, the contents of furniture pieces aren't always emptied out. This is undoubtedly what hap-

LOOMISM
The sentimental value of antiques is truly priceless.

These sporting antiques remind us that price negotiation is a game and never a war.
(Photo courtesy of Shaker Village of Pleasant Hill, Kentucky)

pened. The purse came as a bonus for the winning bidder of the chest of drawers where it had remained all those years.

Sometimes not even a million-dollar piece can bring as much joy as Linda Lee experienced when she rediscovered a childhood keepsake—now a semi-antique/collectible—for a mere $4. Wouldn't Monsieur Renoir be delighted at how much Linda Lee relishes her "déjà vu" purse?

Buy only what makes your heart, eyes, and mind stand up and cheer, such as this English painting of two girls and a dog.

(Photo courtesy of Garth's Auctions, Inc.)

This early 1900s postcard of Chicago is a reminder to keep museums high on your list of "must do" when traveling. The Art Institute of Chicago is in the lower right corner. *(Author's collection)*

Avoid the "C" Word

This charming anecdote about a $4 purse brings up a point about the power of words. By using affirmative terms to refer to your antiques, you imbue them with even more positive energy. When I first started collecting, Aunt Panny taught me to avoid using the word "cheap" to describe our buys. She said, "We may have gotten them for a song, Frankie, but they are not cheap." She told me that to most people, the word "cheap" implies shoddiness or lack of quality, "which isn't the case with our finds," she added.

. . . .

Aunt Panny taught me to avoid using the word "cheap" to describe our buys. She said that the word "cheap" implies shoddiness or lack of quality.

. . . .

Although this entire book focuses on bargains, you can see I followed my aunt's advice and never once used the "c" word. Your antiques will give you much more pleasure if you use sunnier adjectives like inexpensive, affordable, and economical.

WEDGWOOD
ABC

BUT NOT MIDDLE E

By

HARRY M. BUTEN

Never discount the power of books. Always keep learning about antiques.

(Photo courtesy of Skinner's Auction Company)

Your expertise will continue to grow. Soon you will be able to distinguish late 1800s/early 1900s Centennial-type pieces, seen here at Montpelier, from real 1700s versions.

(Photo courtesy of James Madison's Montpelier)

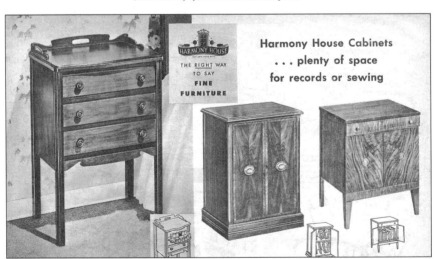

Now you are a real antiquer, meaning you buy something and then find a spot for it when you get home. Remember that de-cluttering rule!

(Author's collection)

Your purchases might not be museum caliber, but they should always be quality. When citing various antiques and semi-antiques/collectibles in this book, I picked only first-class examples to show you how to develop smart buying strategies. The adage "Quality far outlasts the sweetness of price" is true. However, the principles of this book show that we can have both quality and a sweet price. Delete the "c" word from your vocabulary, and you'll enjoy your antiques with greater gusto.

As your knowledge grows, so will your appetite for collecting. English Tea Leaf iron-stone china may one day whet your antiques whistle.

(Photo courtesy of Middletown Journal)

Your purchases might not be museum caliber, but they should always be quality. While "quality far outlasts the sweetness of price," you have learned that we can have both quality and a sweet price.

GRADUATION

At this point, you're ready for your antiques graduation. What a thrilling experience it has been for me to share my Loomisms and prepare you to achieve your antiques dreams. Now that you're finished with this primer, you're about to soar to new heights. Although I can't be with you in person, I will be with you in spirit when you score your first big bargain, bring home the antique of your dreams, or hand someone a gift and say, "It's antique, and I picked it just for you."

Before you remove your cap and gown, I have a surprise for you. Now that you're an antiques jock, I am officially lifting the Antiques Ceiling limiting your purchases to $35 or less when shopping at "Woolworth's." But I want you to keep the other Antiques Ceilings for a while. You'll know when you can dispense with them and let the antiques sky be your limit. Let me bid you a fond farewell by repeating a favorite expression from my NPR radio show: "Keep Antiquing!"

Frank Farmer Loomis IV

Loomisms for Affordable Antiques

Loomisms from Chapter One
- Antiques are far less costly than you ever thought possible.

Loomisms from Chapter Two
- A no-longer-mint, yet quality antique can often be purchased for much less money than if it were still perfect.
- The defects in an antique that seem so serious when shopping appear to fade once they're in your home.
- Antiques affirm the joy of living.

Loomisms from Chapter Three
- Consider anything made before 1920 as antique.

Loomisms from Chapter Five
- The Sensual Approach to Learning will help you become intimately acquainted with antiques. Your eyes, fingers, heart, and even the cushy part of your anatomy will enlighten you.

Loomisms from Chapter Six

- Pine is the Christmas wood because it gives the gift of beauty, practicality, and comfort at an affordable price.

Loomisms from Chapter Seven

- Price negotiation is a sport, not a war. This attitude will help you get the best possible prices for whatever catches your antiques fancy.
- The three negotiation lines combined with honey/gentility, humor, and proper wardrobe are exceptionally effective at lowering prices.
- Buyers respond to charm and humor from the seller, too. Keep that in mind, so you don't get snowed and pay too much.
- At antiques malls, apply the same positive tactics for price negotiation that you use when bartering with a dealer face to face. Your charming approach towards mall employees will help you get friendlier prices.
- Remember, there are many antiques in the sea of life!

Loomisms from Chapter Nine

- You get what you pay for when you buy from first-class dealers, but you won't necessarily pay full price if you've established a good rapport with them.

Loomisms from Chapter Ten

- At antique shows, if you buy from reputable dealers and get it in writing, you can ignore the $35 Antiques Ceiling.
- Arrive at a show shortly after lunch. Take your time to read descriptions and wait until near the end of the show to begin negotiating.

Loomisms from Chapter Eleven

- Limit your purchases to $35 or less on Internet auctions to be safe.
- Never, never say, "I won." You're paying for what you want. Keep this in mind and you'll keep a level head and won't pay more than you intended.
- A few items always fail to bring high bids. This usually happens near the end of an auction, probably because both auctioneer and bidders are getting tired and bored. This is a major budget alert.

Loomisms from Chapter Twelve

- To stretch your purchasing power, avoid trendy antiques and only buy what you like.
- There is no such thing as good taste. It's all subjective.

Loomisms from Chapter Fourteen

- You'll experience great satisfaction when you restore an antique to its former glory

Loomisms from Chapter Fifteen

- Choose Semi-Antiques/Collectible Versions of Classics
- Hang 'em High or From Afar
- Display 'em High
- Buy "Unpedigreed" Paintings for Excellent Savings
- Anonymous Art Is Especially Affordable
- Think Unframed Prints
- Avoid Hometown Antiques
- Provenance Equals Priceyness
- Leave Museum Quality to the Jet Set
- Pass On Pairs
- Avoid Sets
- Unmatched Chairs: Single Is Best

- Give Monogrammed Flatware Your Stamp of Approval
- Worn Carpets Give Deals You Won't Want to Sweep Under the Rug
- Get a Handle on Replaced Handles
- Antiques Unions Are a Match Made in Heaven
- Geography Affects Success

Loomisms from Chapter Sixteen

- We all have impulsive moments for buying things. By choosing antiques as presents, you're filling your hunger for shopping. This good deed saves you from spending unnecessary money and from cluttering your home. Best of all, when gift time arrives, you're ready!
- The odds of giving someone a duplicate gift are much lower because antiques are usually one of a kind.

Loomisms from Chapter Seventeen

- Look for Stangl Pottery.
- Buy Pressed and Molded Glass.
- Stock Up on Linens.
- Serve Up Silver-Plated Flatware.
- Collect Postcards.

Loomisms from Chapter Eighteen

- The sentimental value of antiques is truly priceless.

Bibliography

Adler, Jerry. "The United States of eBay." *Newsweek*, June 17, 2002.

Carron, Christian G. *Grand Rapids Furniture*. Grand Rapids, Mich.: The Public Museum of Grand Rapids, 1998.

Linley, David. *Extraordinary Furniture*. New York: H. N. Abrams, 1996.

Renoir, Jean. *Renoir, My Father*. Boston: Little, Brown and Company, 1958.

INDEX

INDEX